LATE HAVE I LOVED THEE

Stories of Religious Conversion and Commitment in Later Life

Rev. Richard M. Erikson, Ph.D.

PAULIST PRESS
New York/Mahwah, N.J.

The Publisher gratefully acknowledges use of the following material: excerpts from *The Social Construction of Reality: A Treatise in the Sociology of Knowledge*, by Peter Berger and Thomas Luckmann, copyright © 1967, Doubleday, NY, a division of Bantam Doubleday Dell Publishing Group, Inc.

Copyright © 1995 by Richard M. Erikson

Cover art by Cindy Gaudreau

All rights reserved. No part of this book may be reproduced or transmitted in any form or by any means, electronic or mechanical, including photocopying, recording or by any information storage and retrieval system without permission in writing from the Publisher.

Library of Congress Cataloging-in-Publication Data

Erikson, Richard M., 1958-
    Late have I loved thee : stories of religious conversion and commitment in later life / Richard M. Erikson.
      p cm.
    Includes bibliographical references and index.
    ISBN 0-8091-3594-9 (alk. paper)
    1. Catholic converts—United States—Biography. 2. Aged—United States—Religious life. 3. Middle aged persons—United States—Religious life. 4. Catholic Church. Ordo initiationis Christianae adultorum. 5. Initiation rites—Religious aspects—Catholic Church. 6. Catholic Church—United States—Membership. I. Title.
BX4668.A1E75 1995   95-19348
248.2′42′0846—dc20   CIP

Published by Paulist Press
997 Macarthur Boulevard
Mahwah, NJ 07430

Printed and bound in the
United States of America

Contents

LIST OF TABLES v

PREFACE 1

INTRODUCTION 3
    An Overview 6

CHAPTER 1: SETTING THE CONTEXT 9
    Narrative and Life Story in Sociology 9
    Theoretical Foundations 11
    The RCIA Process 20
    Research Design 22
    Religious Conversion 24

CHAPTER 2: STORIES OF
    BIOGRAPHICAL RECONSTRUCTION 30
    Implications of the RCIA Structure
        for Biographical Reconstruction 30
    Biographical Reconstruction Revisited 38
    Biographical Reconstruction Clearly Evident 38
    Biographical Reconstruction Not Strongly Indicated 45
    Biographical Reconstruction Not Evident 50
    Biographical Reconstruction in Process 52
    The Stories of Lifelong Catholics 56
    Conclusion 64

Contents

**CHAPTER 3: BEYOND
    BIOGRAPHICAL RECONSTRUCTION** 68
  Age 69
  Seekers 81
  Crisis or Transition Periods in Life 87
  Early Childhood Memories 94
  Conclusion 102

**CHAPTER 4: FAMILY INFLUENCE AND
    SENSE OF BELONGING** 106
  Family Influence 106
  Sense of Belonging 114
  Conclusion 135

CHAPTER 5: CONCLUSION 139
  Meaning and Belonging 139
  Lessons from the Stories of Older New Catholics ... 142
  Conclusion 151

**APPENDIX A: THE CONFESSIONS OF
    A PRIEST RESEARCHER** 157
  Background 157
  The Reactions of Older New Catholics
      and Prayer Group Members 159
  Personal Reflections 165

**APPENDIX B: THE SAMPLE, THE FIELD SITES, AND
    ROMAN CATHOLICISM AS A CONTEXT** 168
  Overview of the Sample 168
  Field Sites 172
  Why Roman Catholicism? 173

BIBLIOGRAPHY 175

INDEX 192

List of Tables

TABLE 1: Why Do Older People Become Roman Catholic? An Overview 140

TABLE 2: Age of Respondents in Years at Time of Interview 168

TABLE 3: Respondents Married Once 169

TABLE 4: Respondents Married Twice 169

TABLE 5: Self–Reported Income 169

TABLE 6: Self–Reported Level of Educational Attainment 170

TABLE 7: Religion of Early Childhood Household 170

*To my parents,
Rick and Betty Erikson,
who have taught me that it is never too late
to grow in the love and knowledge of God.
And to my brother and sisters,
Ed, Deb and Carol,
who always keep me young at heart.*

Preface

In 1978, as a college sophomore, I read Robert Butler's *Why Survive? Being Old in America* (1976). Butler's book captured my imagination. The study of aging became a passion in my life. Over the past decade and a half I have studied Butler's notion of the life review. Over this time, my conviction has only grown that the life review is a theoretical notion with extraordinary implications for research and for daily life. Butler's advocacy of the importance of listening to life stories has served me well as a sociologist and as a Catholic priest.

I decided to become a Roman Catholic priest in 1982. During my years as a seminary student my love for the study of aging was complemented by another passion, the study of religion. Now, as a sociologist, and particularly in this book, I have been able to merge my passions and to study the religious dynamics involved in the aging process and the aging dynamics involved in the religious process.

In 1988, as a graduate student at the University of Southern California, another book captured my imagination. Berger and Luckmann's *The Social Construction of Reality* (1967) presented a sociological vision that made abundant sense. When I considered their perspectives on religious conversion and community, this study was born. As with Butler's life review, I found in Berger and Luckmann's theoretical perspective practical and research implications. Many of those implications are explored here.

As a priest, I have been involved in the initiation process in the Catholic Church for a decade. I have met a number of people who have become Catholic in later life. In 1987, for example, a seventy-five-year-old man rang the doorbell of a Catholic Church rectory and asked to speak to a priest. When I greeted Mr. Feinstein he told me that he wanted to become a Catholic. As he told the story, the death of a close friend had caused him to consider the meaning of life and death. For a year I listened to Mr. Feinstein's story and accompanied him on his path to Roman Catholicism. The stories that Mr. Feinstein and other older new Catholics told me have fascinated me.

I have found these extraordinary stories of grace, challenge and the quest for God to be captivating for almost every person with whom I have shared them. There are certainly profound lessons for the disciplines of sociology and gerontology, but what makes these stories captivating are the very basic lessons they teach about human, social and religious life.

Through studying the process by which older people have become Roman Catholic, and by listening to their stories, I have been able to merge sociological perspectives that have intrigued me all my adult life. I have been able to bring to sociology a life–story perspective that I find to be extremely relevant to sociological pursuits. I have also been challenged to consider my own journey with God and with God's people.

This book is not only a product of the stories of older new Catholics, but is also a product of my own story. I am grateful to the people who are part of my story, past and present. My mentors, formal and informal, have challenged me to explore the boundaries of my sociological and religious imaginations.

Doctors Jon Miller, Elaine Draper and Don Miller provided invaluable guidance in the researching and writing of this book. Sister Ann Veronica Murphy, S.N.J.M. has been an extraordinary consultant, proofreader, and friend. She personifies for me what it means to age in the Spirit. St. John's Seminaries in Camarillo, California and Brighton, Massachusetts were wonderful communities in which I lived and worked. The participants in the study have revealed to me a view of religious conversion and denominational membership switching that is unprecedented. My family, friends, and church have allowed me to be completely absorbed by the discipline required for this endeavor.

To all those who have contributed to this work, and to those who have contributed to my story, thank you. May God be with you.

Introduction

In Catholic parishes throughout the United States a quiet revolution has begun. Women and men in later life are presenting themselves to the church for membership. Older people seeking membership in the church come from a variety of settings: urban and rural parishes, parishes with state of the art evangelization, parishes staffed with a single priest, parishes largely composed of young families, and from parishes located in the heart of older populations.

What is revolutionary about this phenomenon are the insights on aging and religion revealed in the stories of becoming Catholic in later life. Revolutionary as well are the people and perspectives that older new Catholics represent. These new Catholics represent a dramatic break with the stereotypical view of later life as years when religious change simply does not occur. As our population ages, these new Catholics also represent a present and future challenge to the church. The experiences of older new Catholics in the 1990s speaks to the need for the church, now and in the twenty-first century, to be attentive to the lives and voices of older people.

This revolution is quiet in that, up until now, the numbers of older people seeking membership in the church have been few and their stories have been largely untold. Yet, they depict a revolution that extends beyond the boundaries of parishes and nations. They symbolize people who, in Betty Friedan's words, approach age as an adventure (Friedan, 1993: 571). The shift that Friedan describes in the larger society, from stale images of aging as a time of decline, to vibrant images of aging as a time of new possibilities, is dramatically told in the stories of people who have become Catholic in later life. The amazing people you will be introduced to are living their later years as a time of religious and social renaissance. Society may say they have become Catholic "late" in life, yet, for them, their later years have been the best time to become Catholic.[1] For them, aging in the community of the church has been an adventure.

One of these adventurers is Dot. She is a fifty-nine-year-old college professor who has spent the last several years on sick leave because of recurrent back problems, which have been complicated by a variety of other chronic and acute conditions. When I met her, she wore a long–sleeved shirt to cover the scars that remained from being burned in her childhood. Her husband, formerly the chairperson of the board of directors at a Unitarian church, now, in Dot's words, "has nothing to do with religion." As she welcomed me to her home, she moved slowly and placed herself strategically on a couch. Occasionally, as we talked, she grimaced from the pain. When she told me her age I was shocked. She looked to be a woman who was at least seventy years old.

Despite the physical pain that limits her activities, Dot has just completed the process of becoming Catholic. Her story illustrates the point that answering the question "Why do older people become Roman Catholic?" is a very complex task, but the stories people tell of becoming Catholic are fascinating and informative for ministers of initiation, sociologists, gerontologists, and those captivated by human stories.

In the first question of our interview I asked Dot, "If we could start, then, at the beginning, could you tell me a little bit about where you were born and raised?" She answered with about a ten-minute summary of her life story. She was born into a Methodist family and was raised Methodist. Her mother died when she was two and her father deserted the family. She was raised by her grandfather and step-grandmother. She was married to a non-practicing Jew in a Unitarian ceremony because her husband's family objected to any Christian symbolism. Their two children were raised Unitarian. Both Dot and her husband were active Unitarians during their children's formative years. Dot continues her story:

> So neither of my children was baptized until my daughter converted to Catholicism five or six years ago. We gradually drifted away from the church. For a long while I didn't really miss it; then I started feeling a need for a church family, and I thought about returning to the Methodist Church. I didn't want to go back to the

Unitarian Church. I never felt that it was very spiritual, and I felt that I needed the spiritual side of it. And then my daughter married a Catholic, and after being married for a while she converted to Catholicism and they started inviting me to mass with them. I went regularly, enjoyed what I saw and heard, got more and more interested in it, attended the Inquiry class, more out of curiosity than anything else, and made a lot of friends. I felt connection with the church. So I went on into RCIA, and had my actual confirmation just this last June, but I went through the other steps before.[2]

Dot's description of joining the Catholic Church demonstrates a variety of factors that were evident in many of the stories to be told here. She begins her story of becoming Catholic with her own daughter's becoming Catholic. Family influence was very important for her. Additionally, significant others at the church were influential. As she made "a lot of friends," Dot felt a "connection with the church." Her particular interest in Roman Catholicism finds roots in her curiosity and her spiritual search. Later in our interview Dot said she joined the Inquiry class because "I wanted a church family, I wanted a church association," adding: "Primarily I think I became Catholic because I felt a stronger and stronger need for the spiritual association."

The stories of older new Catholics are compelling human stories, because they detail the search for meaning and belonging among older adults. They are even more compelling given that they are told by people in later life who have joined a mainline religion. The stories of *older* individuals who join *mainline* religions have not been told before. The stories that these older adults tell reveal the human and social nature of joining a religion.

The telling of the stories of our lives is very natural. In the stories we tell we reveal who we perceive, and continually conceive, ourselves to be. In our stories we continually integrate our lives. We discover that the cultural and social milieus in which we live, move, and have our being can at once limit and expand the horizons of our stories. The stories we tell are told and retold. As we age, so do our stories. As we change, so do our stories. Our lives, and our stories, are constantly constructed and reconstructed (Berman, 1991:34). By listening to the stories of people who have become Catholic in later life we will learn how their lives have been constructed and reconstructed in their becoming Catholic.

The source and foundation of this study are the stories of twenty-eight individuals who participated in the process of initiation into the Roman Catholic Church after the age of fifty-eight.[3] The life stories of these individuals result in rich data and attention to the complex personal and social dynamics involved in joining a religion. By my listening to, and retelling, the stories of older new Catholics, theoretical perspectives on religious conversion and membership switching that are relevant to the experiences of these older adults result.

The stories of older new Catholics need to be heard by a variety of professionals. Catechumenate teams need to hear and understand the human journey toward Catholicism. Sociologists need to hear and understand the social aspects of stories of religious change and commitment in later life. Gerontologists need to hear and understand how religious dimensions of life intersect with one's life story. Beyond the professional realm, the stories to be told here contain some very basic and important lessons on living and aging in the Spirit.

AN OVERVIEW

The stories to be told, and the context in which the stories are told, are presented in the following sequence.

Chapter 1 lays the foundations of this study. I will review the place of life stories in sociology and suggest that renewed attention to a life-story approach to sociological investigation is appropriate and beneficial for the discipline of sociology in the 1990s. I will discuss the Rite of Christian Initiation of Adults as a context and I will present the methodology of this study.

Chapter 2 tells the story of biographical reconstruction from the perspective of the older new Catholics. The structural aspects of the RCIA that relate to biographical reconstruction are detailed. Biographical reconstruction is shown to be an important factor in the stories of becoming Catholic. However, unanimous support for past theories of biographical reconstruction is not found.

Chapters 3 and 4 present six other motivating factors for religious conversion and membership switching that emerged from the interviews. Chapter 3 focuses on the four common themes in stories of a personal search for meaning in later life among the older new Catholics:

1) Some older new Catholics came to the Catholic Church after a process of religious seeking; 2) Some stories of becoming Catholic focused on the influence of the aging process and later life; 3) Some people told very dramatic stories of crises or transitions they survived which prompted them to become Catholic; 4) Finally, many people I interviewed linked their becoming Catholic in later life with early childhood memories of Catholicism.

Chapter 4 focuses on the social aspect of becoming Catholic. Family influence is shown to be a very significant factor in the lives of these older adults, and in the decision to become Catholic. The need for a sense of belonging and the social cohesion of the RCIA is also very prominent in the stories of becoming Catholic.

Chapter 5 concludes the study with a call to precision in theoretical reflections on religious conversion and membership switching. The motivating factors present in the life stories of older new Catholics are summarized as relating to the search for meaning and belonging. Biographical accounts and personal narratives are discussed as leading to important theoretical challenges to the monocausal grand theories of religious conversion. By bringing narratives back into sociology I intend to present a dynamic and thorough examination of religious conversion and membership switching in later life. Additionally insights into aging in the Spirit and approaches to the RCIA gleaned from the experience of older new Catholics are presented.

Finally, two appendices deal with specific issues. Appendix A discusses the fact that I am a Catholic priest. The people I interviewed were directly asked to comment on this fact. Their comments are summarized. I also reflect on my role as both a Catholic insider and an outside researcher. Appendix B gives an in-depth view of the methodology of the study.

Notes

1. The title for this book is taken from Book Ten, Chapter 27 of *The Confessions of St. Augustine*. However, even the translations of this popular line from Augustine have different implications. "Late have I loved Thee" is Augustine's assessment of his conversion. Some translations have Augustine writing, "*Too* late have I loved you" (Ryan, 1960:254). The difference implied by the word "too" is subtle, but important. My impression is the new Catholics I spoke with would admit they became Catholic in later life, but they would be hesitant to say they became Catholic *too* late in life.

2. Quotations from the interviews are verbatim quotes except for the removal of incidental verbal utterances such as "uh," "ah," and "um."

3. The process of initiation for adults in the Catholic Church is called The Rite of Christian Initiation of Adults. Some people object to the use of the acronym "RCIA" because acronyms may imply a voluntary organization or a time-specific program. The rites are mandatory and the instructions for initiation are not time specific. The North American Forum on the Catechumenate recommends referring to the initiation rites by ways other than an acronym, such as "the order of Christian Initiation' or "the catechumenal process" (see Oakham, 1993:7–8). The Forum's advocacy of alternatives to "RCIA" is recent and has not yet been widely practiced. The use of "RCIA" in this book refers to the process of initiation as presented in The Rite of Christian Initiation of Adults. No statement is intended regarding its mandatory nature nor its lack of a specific time-line.

1
Setting the Context

I became a sociologist relatively late in my life. I began the study of sociology professionally five years ago, at the age of thirty. My interest in human stories extends as far back as I can remember. As a child I would listen to my grandparents as they told me of distant places. As an adult I have always been intrigued and delighted to hear life stories. In 1988, I began adding the perspective of sociology to my natural inclination toward life stories. The branch of sociology which deals with everyday life spoke to me in very understandable ways about the need for people to tell their stories and the mutual effect of the stories and the social context in which the stories are told. In this chapter I will summarize some of the basic perspectives which sociology brings to the study of life stories. The foundations laid in this chapter help to put the stories of religious change and commitment in later life into a proper context.

NARRATIVE AND LIFE STORY IN SOCIOLOGY

Much has changed since 1918 when Thomas and Znaniecki claimed, "Life records as complete as possible, constitute the *perfect* type of sociological material" (cited in Bertaux, 1981:1). Their book, *The Polish Peasant in Europe and America* (1927), is a foundational work in a personal narrative, life-story or biographical approach to social reality.

A life-story approach to sociology upholds the importance of individual experiences of social reality. Through such means as written autobiographies, oral narratives and group storytelling sessions, sociologists who embrace a life-story approach explore the relationship of individuals and society (Kohli, 1981:63). From this perspective life stories, biographies, and oral histories are always social (Moody, 1988:18).

As the name implies, the stories people tell of their lives are the primary source for life-story study in sociology. Sociologists study life stories in order to understand how societal influences shape the individual and how individual influences relate to society. This book will incorporate a life-story approach which will be complemented by field observations and Catholic initiation documentation.

Those who engage in life-story analysis readily admit that narratives are inherently subjective. The telling of the story may have more impact on an individual's life than an actual event. W.I. Thomas' well-known theorem is called on as a reminder of the importance of subjectivity as social fact: "If men define situations as real, they are real in their consequences" (cited in Elder, 1981:81). A more contemporary effort to put subjectivity into context comes from Denzin: "One becomes the stories one tells" (1989:81).[1]

Although sociology has developed many other perspectives during the twentieth century, the life-story approach continues to be a valuable perspective. The sociology of aging is one subdiscipline which has begun to embrace again the contributions of a life-story approach. The empirical and theoretical benefits of life stories in the sociology of aging are coupled with the fact that individuals need to tell their stories in later life. Personal narrative is well-suited to the study of aging.

In the sociology of religion, life stories have gained renewed interest since Robert Bellah and his associates' well-received portrait of individualism and community in America. In *Habits of the Heart* (1985), the researchers let the narratives of the people they interviewed tell the story of middle-class America's lack of a vocabulary to make sense of society and themselves. In the sociology of religious conversion the personal accounts of converts have been prominent in research and theory building.

In his 1964 American Sociological Association address, George Homans urged sociologists to "bring men back in." I am so convinced of the importance of life stories for understanding social reality that I would like sociologists to "bring narration back in." The approach of this project in discovering why older individuals are becoming

Catholic is well-stated in Berger and Berger's handbook on sociology, *Sociology: A Biographical Approach:*

> If one is to understand what goes on in a particular social situation, then one must understand how the participants in that situation make sense of it, what their motives and intentions are and how they judge the moral implications of what they and others are doing (1972:336).

THEORETICAL FOUNDATIONS

The primary goal of this book is to examine various personal and social motivating factors for individuals who become Roman Catholic in later life. Chief among the motivating factors to be examined is biographical reconstruction.[2] In this discussion I will apply theoretical insights from gerontology and the sociology of conversion to the experience of people who have become Roman Catholic in later life.

Gerontologists discuss the search for meaning in later life and the inevitable developmental tasks posed through purposeful reminiscence (Butler, 1963). Sociologists of conversion discuss biographical reconstruction as an indicator of conversion (Berger and Luckmann, 1967; Snow and Machalek, 1983). At the outset of this study I assumed these two strands of theory and research would be linked in the experience of later-life Catholics. That is, through becoming Catholic, older individuals would discover added meaning in their lives and find a context in which to put their life stories in order.

Sociological Perspectives on Religious Conversion

At the turn of the century William James favorably quoted a psychology of religion professor in stating, "Conversion is in its essence a normal adolescent phenomenon, incidental to the passage from the child's small universe to the wider intellectual and spiritual life of maturity" (James, 1961:167). Over the course of the twentieth century, the overwhelming majority of studies about the religious conversion process have focused on adolescence and non-mainline religions. Theoretical explanations of conversion in adolescence and young adulthood, which focus largely on intermarriage and the family life cycle, have not been explored in relation to later life.[3] To my knowledge, no other study has specifically examined religious conversion and membership switching in later life.

An Introduction to Biographical Reconstruction

A review of conversion and life-review literature has led to the expectation that, in the experience of older adults, what has been called "the ordering of biographies" (Berger and Luckmann, 1967), "the social construction of the past" (Taylor, 1978) and "biographical reconstruction" (Snow and Machalek, 1983) will be demonstrated. Despite the many and varied theories on conversion, almost all accounts agree that the conversion experience is indicated by converts in the retelling of their life stories through the newly acquired social and personal context of being a convert. A typical expression of the reconstruction of one's life story, after a conversion experience, is the sentence, "At the time I *thought*...but now I *know*" (Berger and Luckmann, 1967:160).

Basing the notion of biographical reconstruction on the work of William James, David Snow and Richard Machalek suggest that all conversions involve a division between an individual's past and present (1983:266). The past is radically reinterpreted and reorganized through the newly acquired meaning of conversion and newly acquired social type of being a convert. One's biography is reconstructed based on the fact that one is a convert.

Biographical reconstruction is not restricted to converts. Yet the experience of a religious conversion is so important in the life of a convert that everything else in life is understood and experienced through the prism of conversion. Looking back and putting one's life in order is a common human experience, but because converts have a new and dramatic frame of reference in their lives, looking back and putting their lives in order happens in a more intensive and deliberate way (Snow and Machalek, 1983:269; Snow and Phillips, 1980:431).[4] One woman I interviewed captured the essence of biographical reconstruction when she compared her pre-Catholic life to her present Catholic life saying, "I feel I'm an entirely different person now than I was then."

Snow and Machalek argue that biographical reconstruction, and three other rhetorical features (adoption of a master attribution scheme, suspension of analogical reasoning, and embracing a master role) mark the occasion of conversion. Yet their research was based only on the study of one religious movement—The Nichiren Shoshu Buddhists of

America. Staples and Mauss (1987) applied Snow and Machalek's model in a study of fifteen Christian evangelical college students. They found all four rhetorical indicators in their sample of converts. However, when comparisons were made with lifelong Christians, only biographical reconstruction was found to be unique to those who claimed to have had a conversion experience. Lifelong Christians were more likely to refer to personal change as "growth," or "a process," whereas converts indicated a clean break with the past. Staples and Mauss suggest that the other three rhetorical indicators (other than biographical reconstruction) are equally as relevant for religious commitment as they are for religious conversion.[5]

The Life Review Process

Although the notion of biographical reconstruction in converts derives primarily from research on adolescent and young adult converts, the expectation of this research is that older new Catholics will indicate an even greater emphasis on biographical reconstruction than younger converts. This contention is based on research on aging which discusses the inevitable need in later life to order one's biography. At the forefront of the literature on the reordering of personal biography is the notion of life review.

Dr. Robert Butler introduced the concept of the life review about thirty years ago. Over the past three decades life reviews among older people have received extensive attention, especially in the study of the psychology of aging. Butler described the life review as a natural, universal process of looking back at the past. The focus of the review is on unresolved conflicts. These conflicts are reviewed and integrated into one's life story. Butler suggested that the life review is prompted by the realization of the possibility of physical decline in later life and of death. The contemporary experience of the individual shapes the life review as does the character the person has developed throughout his/her life. Butler considered the life review to be a positive and therapeutic developmental stage of growth. He suggested that the life review process

> ...helps account for the increased reminiscence in the aged, that it contributes to the occurrence of certain late-life disorders, particularly depression, and that it participates in the evolution of

such characteristics as candor, serenity, and wisdom among certain of the aged (1963:65).

Reminiscence plays a central role in the life-review process, yet the life review incorporates far more than simple reminiscence.[6] The aged are not only taking stock of themselves as they review their lives, but are also projecting what remains for them to do in the future, and what material and emotional legacies they may have to give to others. The life review is usually initiated in an intensive way in early old age. Yet, for some, initiation is delayed. Some individuals never accomplish the task of personality integration presented by the life review.

The life review can, and does, occur at all stages of life, but in later life the frequency and urgency of the task is increased, because of the actual nearness of life's termination, the increased time for self-reflection, the removal of customary defenses provided for by work, and many other of the usual accompaniments to aging.

The life review often focuses on painful and difficult aspects of a person's life. Although personality integration is often the result of the life review, Butler also suggests that individuals can engage in the life review in a way that is detrimental to personality integration. He writes:

> The most tragic situation is that of the person whose increasing—but only partial—insight leads to a sense of total waste: The horrible insight just as one is about to die of feeling that one has never lived, or of seeing oneself realistically as in some sense inadequate (1963:69).

Much of the anxiety present in the review process, which may lead to depression and/or despair, is focused on unresolved conflicts. Generally, the more intense these are, the more work remains to be accomplished toward reintegration. If unresolved conflicts are successfully reintegrated into one's life and life story, then a new significance and meaning can be discovered in one's life. Preparation for death and mitigation of fears may follow (Butler, 1975:413). Butler suggests that "a constructive reevaluation of the past may facilitate a serene and dignified acceptance of death" (1963:73).

The primary goal of the life review is to identify areas of conflict and concern, with accompanying guilt and fears, and to eventually resolve these, bringing about a reintegration within a person's consciousness (Morycz, 1980:382). A positive psychotherapeutic function is involved, which includes the processes of resolving, reorganizing, and reintegrating.

Creen and Simmons write:

> The aging person needs to come to grips with his life as a *totality*; the integrity-despair crisis must be resolved. Through the life review process the aging person, in reconsidering his life and re-evaluating his actions, forms his thoughts of himself into a unity (1977:277).

Critics of life review (including the late Simone de Beauvoir) reject the claim that the life review is a natural means of psychological integration. Instead, they suggest that the real challenge of old age lies not in turning inward and toward the past but in turning outward in an activist mode. The life review is presented from this viewpoint as an obstacle to an individual's quest to realize his/her potential (Moody, 1988:10). Wallace (1992:120-121) has suggested that Butler's emphasis on the natural and inner nature of the life review is misguided. Rather, the life review is essentially a social activity that is prompted by social interaction.

Butler's claim that the life review is a universal process for all elderly people has also been criticized. Sharan Merriam reported on a study focused on centenarians. The study challenged the universality of the life review and the linking of the life review with age and approaching death (Merriam, 1993:173). Similarly, Lamme and Baars reported "...results from empirical studies show that not all elderly people are intensely preoccupied with their past and that if they are, this behavior hardly ever matches the structure of the life review as described by Butler" (Lamme and Baars, 1993:300).

Despite these critiques, the life review has been overwhelmingly received as a valuable and practical insight into the aging process. Recently attention has been given to the religious implications of the process. Since the *Journal of Religion and Aging* was founded in 1985, (now retitled the *Journal of Religious Gerontology*) the life review has been a constant theme. Such articles as "Life Review: A Report of the Effectiveness of a Structured Life Review Process" (Haight, 1989b) have spoken to the relevance of the life review for theory and practice.

The life review has been addressed in the social sciences almost exclusively as a psychological process. By linking life-review literature with the sociology of conversion literature, the sociological significance of converts' reconstructions of the past will be shown.

General Theoretical Foundation: Berger and Luckmann

The theoretical foundations for this research are not limited to gerontology and the sociology of conversion. Sociological theory in general provides a context for this research. Our focus on the social reconstruction of the past in the conversion process finds its theoretical roots in the framework of the social construction of reality as presented by Berger and Luckmann (1967).

One of the primary tasks of sociology is to put human action into social context. This is precisely the task that Berger and Luckmann embrace in their 1966 work, *The Social Construction of Reality*. In putting human action into context, the authors borrow freely from such sociological masters as Weber (emphasis on subjective meaning), Durkheim (the nature of social reality), Mead (notion of the dialectic, social-psychology presuppositions), and Schutz (general phenomenological approach). The title of their treatise reveals the central theme: reality is socially constructed. The basic questions that frame Berger and Luckmann's treatment of the sociology of knowledge are: What is real? and, How is one to know?

Berger and Luckmann speak of the social nature of reality construction. They argue that one's self-image is socially constructed. The ordering of biography takes place in a social context. One's life story is reshaped in and through a group or in and through one's significant others.

Berger and Luckmann contend that everyday life presents itself as a reality that women and men must interpret. Interpretation takes place in a social context and always reflects the subjective experience of the individual. Each of us, in our own way, seeks to make sense of the reality we experience, and we shape that reality into a meaningful and coherent whole. Part of the task of the life review, and presumably of the reconstruction of one's biography in the conversion process, is "to make sense" of one's experience. The reviewer or convert is seeking to shape his/her life story into a coherent whole.

Berger and Luckmann's notion of the "ordering of biography"

captures the essence of the life review. In the ordering of biography, "the totality of the individual's life...must be made subjectively meaningful" (p. 92). The search for meaning is at the center of the life-review process and, once again, presumably at the center of the conversion process.

Dealing with memories in one's life is a key element in the ordering of one's biography. Yet, similar to the life review, recollections of past memories must be complemented by life preview. Three modes of time are addressed by the individual. The individual looks back at his/her past, finds meaning for the present, and hope for the future. Berger and Luckmann address a "radical reinterpretation" of one's past which parallels Butler's notion:

> Since it is relatively easier to invent things that never happened than to forget those that actually did, the individual may fabricate and insert events wherever they are needed to harmonize the remembered with the reinterpreted past. Since it is the new reality rather than the old that now appears dominatingly plausible to him, he may be perfectly "sincere" in such a procedure—subjectively, he is not telling lies about the past but bringing it in line with the truth that, necessarily, embraces both present and past (Berger and Luckmann, 1967:160).

Personal grappling with issues of mortality, finitude and death is a major motivating factor for the life review in later life. Berger and Luckmann, in a related concept, speak of the temporal structure of everyday life. Each person is born on a certain day, into a certain time. The location of each individual in a temporal sphere decisively shapes his/her situation (p. 28). Berger and Luckmann suggest that by temporal awareness *alone* the individual reenters the reality of everyday life.

Berger and Luckmann's recognition of the importance of modes of time for the individual and for society has been lacking in social theory in general. Much of social theory has focused on the "here and now." Berger and Luckmann, combined with Butler, represent a challenge for a broad view of temporal realities in social theory.

The definition of subjective reality by the individual is subject to constant modification and transformation. Since reality is socially constructed, alternative definitions of reality may threaten one's core perception of reality. Thus, social factors that seem to give legitimacy to one's subjective definition of reality are essential. These suggestions of Berger and Luckmann at once account for the possibility of conversion (modification and transformation of one's subjective reality, especially the past) and the potential impact of the group into which the new Catholic is socialized (see RCIA description below).

A study of the social reconstruction of the past in the conversion process, which includes macro-sociological analysis, has the potential both to contribute to an area in social psychology which has been lacking and to provide theoretical and empirical content to a critiqued area of Berger and Luckmann's thought. (For example, see Ritzer, in Snizek, 1979:39.) An empirical approach to Berger and Luckmann's theory is long overdue.

Berger and Luckmann on Religious Conversion

Berger and Luckmann discuss religious conversion as an example of how reality can be transformed for and/or by an individual. They suggest that the religious conversion experience "involves a reinterpretation of past biography *in toto*" (1967:160). The present interpretive scheme of conversion is applied to one's past. New motives are understood and assigned. Such statements as, "I already knew then in an unclear manner..." and "I really did this because..." are indicative of the reinterpretation which results from the conversion experience. Not only is the total biography of an individual reordered, specific events and persons of past significance are reinterpreted. Berger and Luckmann call this process a "re-socialization" of the past in which "the past is reinterpreted to conform to the present reality, with the tendency to retroject into the past various elements that were subjectively unavailable at the time" (1967:163).

Not surprisingly, given Berger and Luckmann's use of George Herbert Mead, their notion of re-socialization of the past is similar to notions presented in Mead's *Philosophy of the Present* (1932) whereby personal biographies are constantly redefined in the light of new experience (Snow and Machalek, 1983:269). In discussing Meadian social psychology, Straus suggests that, although Mead recognized the complex interaction between active individuals and their constraining environments, social scientists have largely ignored the fact that "people make circumstances just as much as circumstances make people" (1976:270). He suggests that, as a social process, socialization must be "stood on its head." He concludes: "The interesting and appropriate question becomes not how do groups metabolize human beings, but how do individuals generate, operate, and use their groups in the continuous creation of their lives" (1976:271). This project will respond to Straus' plea, and Berger and Luckmann's perspective, through a careful analysis of how the RCIA process, and the Catholic Church in general, is used by older new Catholics in the reconstruction of their past.

Finally, Berger and Luckmann's emphasis on the importance of significant others in reality maintenance is echoed in conversion literature. Recent studies have increasingly presented conversion as "a process of coming to see that reality is what one's friends claim it to be. The new self of the convert is defined in terms of the reference group that is being joined" (Duggan, 1984b:128). As will be discussed below, a comparison group of lifelong Catholics will provide the opportunity to compare a long-term Catholic reference group with the RCIA reference groups.

Theoretical Summary

In brief, sociological theories of religious conversion, based on research primarily in adolescence and young adulthood, have suggested that biographical reconstruction is a motivator for, and/or a result of, religious conversion. Parallels to biographical reconstruction are found in the research on aging. Butler contends that the life review, which is one aspect of biographical reconstruction, is an inevitable developmental task to be engaged in in later life. The motivating factors for the life review are dealing with unresolved conflicts in one's life, facing issues of death and immortality, and addressing increased reminiscence in later life.

In this book we will explore the relationship of biographical reconstruction and religious conversion in later life. A review of past theory and research leads to the expectation that some older adults resolve the issues posed by the life review and biographical reconstruction through religious conversion and/or through denominational membership switching, or that religious conversion and/or joining a new religion prompt an increased engagement in the life review and eventual biographical reconstruction by the older adult. Furthermore, this research will explain if, and how, the RCIA process provides a social structure for the religious conversion experience and the reconstructed biography.

THE RCIA PROCESS

Berger and Luckmann argue that reality is maintained in consciousness by a social process. Significant others play a central role in the maintenance of reality. The authors write: "To have a conversion experience is nothing much. The real thing is to be able to keep on taking it seriously; to retain a sense of its plausibility. *This* is where the religious community comes in. It provides the indispensable plausibility structure for the new reality" (1967:158).

The new Catholics interviewed for this study all have participated in the Rite of Christian Initiation of Adults. Presumably, in presenting themselves as candidates for baptism, potential Catholics are at least willing to assume the role of a convert. The RCIA process provides the "indispensable plausibility structure" for the convert, that is, the process gives meaning, purpose and legitimacy to religious conversion. Presumably the RCIA process will serve as a plausibility structure for the reconstruction of one's past. Because a formal social structure is involved in the conversion process, and because being a convert entails the social acceptance of a new role and new meaning, we can speak of a "*social* reconstruction of one's biography."

In 1950, the number of American converts to Roman Catholicism per 1,000 active Catholics was 4.3. In 1980, just before the implementation of the RCIA in many United States parishes, the number of converts per 1,000 active Catholics had dropped to 1.6. With the implementation of the RCIA, one key Catholic evangelization leader set the goal of 10 converts per 1,000 active Catholics in the 1990s. The hope of church leaders is to have 500,000 converts per year in the 1990s (Hoge, 1981:174).[7]

Many of the adults who are baptized or received into full communion in the Catholic Church do so through the RCIA process. National and local statistics on new members in the Catholic Church are not broken down into age groups. From parish and diocese samples we can assume the percentage of those who become Catholic after the age of fifty-five is small.

The RCIA process is the formal procedure and ceremony of admittance to the Catholic Church for adults. Most adults who become

Catholic do so through this standardized instructional and ritual process for becoming a full member of the Catholic Church. The Latin text was released on January 6, 1972. Over the past decade the rite has become widely practiced in Catholic parishes in the United States. In the Los Angeles archdiocese there is a Coordinator for the Rite of Christian Initiation of Adults on the archdiocesan level and a director in 230 of 285 Catholic parishes.

The RCIA consists of four periods (Mick, 1989:55f):

(1) The precatechumenate is a period of inquiry, evangelization, and introduction to Catholicism. The Rite of Acceptance makes the participants members of the church, not as baptized Catholics (full members of the church), but as members of the Order of Catechumenate.

(2) The catechumenate proper may last several years. This is a time of catechesis and formation. The catechumenate ends with Rite of Election or enrollment of names for the Easter sacraments. The importance of the Rite of Election is indicated by the fact that the ceremony ought to be conducted by the local bishop. The rite indicates the church's judgment that the catechumens are ready to be baptized at the most important liturgy in the Catholic yearly calendar.

(3) Purification and enlightenment consists of an intense time of spiritual growth and preparation for the sacraments. Public scrutinies (instructions and promises) occur for three weeks before baptism. At the climactic liturgy (the Easter vigil), the RCIA participants become full members of the church and receive the Rites (sacraments) of Initiation.

(4) The mystagogy, or postbaptismal catechesis, takes place for fifty days after the completion of the Rites of Initiation. This period is designed to facilitate full entrance into Catholic life. Despite local parish variations on time and teaching material, each parish is expected to follow this standardized four-step procedure.[8]

The RCIA has been described in Catholic literature as "a model for all adult growth and conversion" (Dunning, 1979:153). The RCIA is remarkable in that *adult* conversion is viewed as normative. Yet adult conversions to Roman Catholicism have occurred throughout the history of the church. The focus of the process on the adult results in a structure which seeks to be attentive to adult needs, expressions, and transitions. Dunning writes, "The process begins with autobiography, sharing our personal pilgrimage, especially the important events in that journey. This leads to a questioning, an inquiry, a search for the meaning and significance of our lives" (1979:143). Dunning's description of the RCIA explicitly links the process with the life review. Furthermore, Dunning's comments suggest that the life review in the RCIA process occurs on a personal and collective level.

RESEARCH DESIGN

The core of this study is narratives obtained from intensive interviews with older individuals who have participated in the RCIA in Southern California. A list of over ninety individuals over the age of fifty-eight who have become Catholic in the Archdiocese of Los Angeles and the Diocese of Fresno was compiled from the RCIA directors in each parish. All but one participant were referred to me by a local parish RCIA director.[9] From the list of new Catholics the interview sample was chosen based on diversity in geographical setting, gender, age (young-old to old-old), marital status, and length of involvement in the RCIA process.

The twenty-eight participants went through the RCIA in fifteen different Catholic parishes within a two-hundred-mile radius of downtown Los Angeles. They came from urban, suburban, and desert communities. They became involved with the RCIA mainly through reading about it in the parish bulletin, being invited by someone, or personally contacting the church to seek membership. Two individuals were still in the preparation for membership process when they were interviewed. The other participants had become Catholic as recently as nine days before the interview, and as long ago as when the first RCIA group in the Archdiocese of Los Angeles became members of the Catholic Church, in 1981. Appendix B presents an in-depth analysis of the background of the people who participated in this study.

One amazing coincidence is present among the people I interviewed. Lenny and Ted were both born in 1912 in the same Midwest state. Both moved to the same Southern California neighborhood. Both married Catholic women and eventually attended the same Catholic church regularly with their wives. Both enrolled in the same RCIA program. They became Catholic one year apart at the ages of sixty-eight and sixty-nine, respectively. I interviewed them five days apart. Neither Ted nor Lenny mentioned each other. Because of the confidentiality promised to each person I interviewed, I could not ask if they knew each other, or if they knew of the remarkable similarity in their life stories. Indeed, the similarity in their stories emerged only during the second interview and was confirmed in the analysis of the data.[10]

In addition to intensive interviews, I observed several RCIA meetings, rites, and training sessions at various levels and moments in the process. (See Appendix B for a complete list of field sites.) I was particularly interested in documenting the ways in which group interaction and the content of teaching materials did, or did not, provide a context for the RCIA participant's reconstructed biography and for the religious conversion experience and/or membership switching.

Comparison Group

Although sociology of conversion literature agrees that biographical reconstruction is a prime indicator of a conversion experience, sociologists have not adequately described or accounted for *how* the biographical reconstruction of converts differs from the biographical reconstruction which is a normal aspect of the developmental tasks of aging (Heirich 1977:657). Thus, a comparison group for this research is a group of lifelong Catholics. I conducted intensive, qualitative life-review interviews with six elderly women participants of a prayer group in a Roman Catholic parish west of Los Angeles. The perspectives from these interviews will be compared with the perspectives from interviews with the RCIA participants to establish how, and in what ways, the biographical reconstruction of new Catholics differs from the biographical reconstruction of lifelong Catholics.

In addition to the comparisons provided in the interview data, I observed fifteen weekly meetings of the prayer group and a final meeting months later when the prayer group disbanded. There are many structural parallels that result in the prayer group being an appropriate group for comparison. Both the prayer group and RCIA meetings share the following characteristics: regularly scheduled weekly meetings, procedures which encourage individual sharing of life stories, close attachment to and dependence on a group leader, personal bonding among members, and bringing life experiences in dialogue with religious beliefs. The prayer group differs from most RCIA groups in that it is composed of all women and all members are individuals over the age of seventy. One of the members of the prayer group became

Catholic in the 1970s. Her reflections will provide a link between those who joined the church in later life and the lifelong Catholics. Finally, both the RCIA groups and the prayer group experienced termination. The RCIA process ends naturally with the liturgy of initiation. The prayer group ended when the religious sister who facilitated the group retired. The comparison group data are presented as exploratory findings suggestive of further research. Selective comparisons will be drawn throughout this study to help highlight some important similarities and differences in the experience and stories of the two groups.

RELIGIOUS CONVERSION

In general, sociologists have studied religious conversion under three categories (Snow and Machalek, 1984:171f) : (1) Membership status refers to shifts in church organizational affiliation. But this may mistakenly equate religious conversion with a change in membership status; (2) Demonstration events refer to public displays of conversion that function as status confirmation rituals. But demonstration events may be indicative of compliance to normative pressures rather than internal change. Religious conversion cannot be inferred from demonstration events; (3) Rhetorical indicators refer to linguistic patterns that indicate a conversion experience. These linguistic patterns are demonstrated in the four rhetorical properties mentioned above: biographical reconstruction, adoption of a master attribution scheme, suspension of analogical reasoning, and embracing of the convert role. Yet these rhetorical indicators have not been explored extensively.

The participants in this study are all individuals who: (1) have been accepted, or are in the process of being accepted, as full members of the Roman Catholic Church (membership); and (2) have taken part in the Rite of Christian Initiation of Adults or some variant thereof (demonstration event).

The third indicator of conversion (rhetoric) has required special attention in this research. Some Catholics who are accepted for full membership in the church, and who participate in the RCIA, have not had a religious conversion. For example, an individual who becomes Catholic to please his/her spouse would not fit into Snow and Machalek's third indicator of conversion unless a personal religious conversion is indicated as well.

An additional problem is defining a personal religious conversion. Each person I interviewed was asked: "Have you ever had what you would describe as a religious conversion?" An affirmative answer to this question will be the indicator of a religious conversion. The wording of this question intends to discover the individual's perception of the presence or absence of a religious conversion in her/his personal story.[11]

Even though many people I interviewed talked openly and directly about religious conversion, some people had definitive notions of religious conversion that would exclude such an occurrence in their own life. For example, some spoke of the Protestant practice of altar calls and immediate and identifiable change, saying that was not their experience. One man said, "When I hear the word 'conversion,' I think you are an atheist one day and the next day you're Christian. And to me I was never an atheist. I was always, you know, a Christian." Another man, when asked if he ever had a religious conversion, replied, "Well, you mean like a Holy-Roller-type thing?"

Thus one lesson from the reflections of those interviewed is the need for far more critical analysis of the use of the term "religious conversion" in sociological literature and the need for far more nuanced analysis of interdenominational differences in approaches to religious conversion.

Additionally, important distinctions need to be drawn between religious experience, religious conversion, and denominational membership switching. A religious experience is present when an individual has what that person would describe as an encounter with the transcendent. Examples of a religious experience include claims to have heard the voice of God, dubbing some event in one's life "a miracle," or describing a dead person present in an other-worldly form.

A religious conversion involves an identifiable change in a person's religious perceptions or attitude. Religious conversions can be sudden or gradual. Religious conversions may, or may not, include a religious experience. An example of a religious conversion which was prompted by a religious experience comes from a seventy-one-year-old woman who told of an experience she had as a teenager in a youth camp. She was addressing the question, "Have you ever had what you would describe as a religious conversion?"

> Well, I was there one night, and I woke up in the middle of the night and I swear to God there was a white entity sitting in the

> chair next to the bed. And I got so frightened I pulled the covers up quick.
>
> *This was during your Methodist retreat?*
>
> Yeah.
>
> *Yeah.*
>
> Well, then I got brave and pulled the covers down and it was gone. And I was shaken up for a week over that because I figured in my mind I really saw something there. I don't know to this day if I did or didn't. But maybe it was an angel. I think it maybe—might of been. But at that time I—I became even more sure that I...wanted to be more religious, so to speak.

In this exchange Judy indicates that her perception of a white entity (religious experience) led to wanting to be "more religious" (religious conversion).

Denominational membership switching involves a change in religious affiliation from one religious organization to another. This change many involve moving from non-participation in one denomination to an active membership status in another denomination. Denominational switching is relatively common. As many as fifty percent of adult Protestants have indicated a different denominational preference than they did as children (Hadaway, 1978:322; Roof and McKinney, 1987). A change in denominational membership may or may not include a religious experience and/or a religious conversion. For example, denominational membership switching where a religious experience or conversion is not present occurs when people do not find their own denomination when they move and so join another denomination.

The issue is complicated further by the use of the word "convert." Sociologically, "convert" is often used to categorize an individual who has simply changed denominational membership. The use of the word "convert" in this study *does not* presume that an individual has had a religious conversion.

Additionally, the Catholic Church upholds a distinct definition of a convert. The RCIA process often includes three groups: baptized Christians (called candidates), baptized Catholics who were never raised as Catholic (formerly called uncatechized persons), and unbaptized adults (called catechumens). Those who were previously baptized are never referred to as catechumens or converts (Mick, 1989:25–26). The participants in this study include catechumens and candidates. For the purposes of this study some individuals will be called converts who, the Catholic Church would insist, in name, are not.

Finally, stories of conversion are not fixed descriptions of a past occurrence (Beckford, 1978). Rather, the stories are constructions and reconstructions of experiences which are informed and influenced by current occurrences. Thus converts' stories of conversion may differ if they are given the day after a conversion experience as opposed to, say, ten years after the event. Additionally, the conversion stories are retrospective. The stories are not precise descriptions of a conversion process or event as it happened. Rather, the stories are a subjective retelling of the experience. This issue was addressed, in part, by my interviewing older individuals who were enrolled in the RCIA program but who were not yet baptized. In an ideal research world I would be able to interview individuals who are in the midst of a biographical reconstruction and who have not yet decided to convert. Current RCIA candidates appeared to be the closest subjects to this ideal.[12]

Throughout this project, when people were told of the nature of this study, their reaction was usually twofold: (1) Identifying the study of older new Roman Catholics to be "interesting." "How interesting!" was a typical response; (2) Asking, "Are there any older converts to study?" My answer to the first reaction was to affirm the basic attraction, interest, and even fascination I found in the topic. My answer to the second reaction was, "Well, there are *enough* older converts to study." Religious conversion and membership switching in later life is an unusual occurrence. Yet, through the RCIA, and through the list of older new Catholics provided by RCIA directors, we certainly have *enough* to study.

The perspectives on religious change and commitment summarized in this chapter seem to present much support for the expectation that older new Catholics would give strong indications of life review and biographical reconstruction in their stories of becoming Catholic. Surprisingly this is not the case. Chapter 2 tells of the place of life review and biographical reconstruction in the stories of becoming

Catholic in later life. Chapters 3 and 4 bring us beyond biographical reconstruction to other factors which are just as important in the lives of older new Catholics.

Notes

1. The subjective nature of storytelling is recognized by one man who told me, "We probably say the same things too often. Old folks do that. [laughing] You know, we can make the story bigger and better...."

2. An argument could be made that biographical reconstruction should more appropriately be called *autobiographical* reconstruction. The reconstruction is primarily the effort of the individual creating and re-creating her/his own story. However, the use of the word "biographical" is established in literature. And the use of the word "biographical" may allow more room for the inclusion of personal and social influences outside the control of the individual. Thus, I will continue the use of the term "biographical reconstruction."

3. For an overview of the focus of research on religious conversion in the adolescent years see Gillespie's *The Dynamics of Religious Conversion*, 1991. After surveying studies of religious conversion since 1899, Gillespie concludes, "Studies using empirical methods have tended to agree as to adolescence being a prominent scene for conversion" (p. 98). One study which addressed age differences in conversion is Suchman's "Analyzing the Determinants of Everyday Conversion" (1992:S23).

4. Snow and Machalek have been criticized because they give no indication as to how to decide how much reconstruction is beyond normal (Staples and Mauss, 1987:136).

5. Staples and Mauss' interpretation differs from other researchers who suggest that biographical reconstruction is a *result of*, and not a *motivation for*, conversion. Snow and Machalek assume that biographical reconstruction is a result of conversion. Viewing biographical reconstruction as a motivation for conversion is in line with the perspective of Roger Straus, who describes conversion as a desired means of self-change and life-change (1976:252). He links conversion directly with "the quest to change one's life" (p. 269).

6. The following description of the life review is based on the descriptions of the life review as presented in the various references of Butler listed in the Bibliography.

7. For the calendar year 1993, the Archdiocese of Los Angeles, composed of 3,559,816 Catholics, reported 89,122 infant baptisms, 2,198 adult baptisms and 1,620 individuals received into full communion with the Catholic Church. For 1993, the Diocese of Fresno, composed of 353,400 Catholics, reported 16,532 infant baptisms, 558 adult baptisms, and 629 individuals received into full communion with the Catholic Church (*The*

Official Catholic Directory: Anno Domini, 1994:527, 361). "Individuals received into full communion with the Catholic Church" refers to those individuals who were previously baptized in another Christian denomination. The Catholic Church does not "re-baptize" when the validity of a baptism is recognized.

8. The acceptance of the RCIA process in the Catholic Church has not been unanimous. Some parishes have refused to implement the program because of lack of staff or disagreement with the nature of the process. Andrew Greeley suggests that the social and structural aspects of the RCIA have become oppressive. He argues, "In the hands of its enthusiasts, the R.C.I.A. has become a hammer and the presumably Spirit-less laity—Catholic or would-be Catholic—have become nails" (1989:231).

9. A priest referred me to a former Presbyterian and Episcopal minister who met with the priest alone, following an RCIA-based catechesis.

10. Lenny's and Ted's parallel lives personify Karl Mannheim's words: "Individuals who belong to the same generation, who share the same year of birth, are endowed, to that extent, with a common location in the historical dimension of the social process" (cited in Myerhoff, 1980:134).

11. The decision to have the people I interviewed themselves tell if they have had a religious conversion or not is reflective of the same decision made by Staples and Mauss: "Because we view conversion as an inherently subjective phenomenon, we believe that the subject, and only the subject, is qualified to tell us who he or she *really* is" (1987:138). Wayne Proudfoot reached a similar conclusion in his survey of religious experience: "The distinguishing mark of a religious experience is not the subject matter but the kind of explanation the subject believes is appropriate" (1985:231).

12. The subjective retelling of one's story is proper data for study. The objective reality of the events in a person's life is not as significant in the study of biographical reconstruction (and conversion) as are the roles those events played in reshaping a person's life and the place they have acquired in the individual's memory. In many ways the place the conversion stories have played in the weaving of one's life is as important, if not more important, than the actual conversion moment or process.

2
Stories of Biographical Reconstruction

This chapter examines biographical reconstruction in the stories of older new Catholics. Prior to this examination, an overview of the implications of the RCIA structure on biographical reconstruction will help put the stories into perspective.

IMPLICATIONS OF THE RCIA STRUCTURE FOR BIOGRAPHICAL RECONSTRUCTION

The RCIA is a social structure with international, national, regional, and local manifestations. Internationally, Catholic churches throughout the world are mandated to follow the *Rite of Christian Initiation of Adults* "revised by Decree of the Second Vatican Ecumenical Council and Published by Authority of Pope Paul VI" (*Rite,* 1988). Nationally, "The North American Forum on the Catechumenate" serves as a resource and as a source of advocacy regarding RCIA issues. This grassroots movement consists of parish ministers and professional catechists. Regionally, bishops seek to implement and monitor the RCIA. Locally, each Catholic parish in the United States is *mandated* by the National Catholic Conference of Bishops to implement the RCIA.

The influence of this social structure is ever present. For example, on September 5, 1991, Cardinal Roger Mahony wrote a letter to every priest in the Archdiocese of Los Angeles. In the letter he stated:

> I am aware that implementation of the Rite of Christian Initiation of Adults as the mandated normative way of initiating adults and

children of catechetical age is considered by some to be optional. *This is not so.* Traditional inquiry programs or weekly adult education sessions are seen by some as adequate. These, however, lack the liturgical and community aspects integral to the full formation of new members for active participation in the life and ministry of the church, and do not respond to the mandate given by the NCCB to the RCIA.

In the course of this study I have observed RCIA meetings and training sessions at various parishes and levels of the Archdiocese of Los Angeles and Diocese of Fresno. Such diverse field settings were chosen to gain a sense of the sweeping nature of the RCIA structure and how it is manifested. The end result of these observations is an awareness of the rigor and purpose of the RCIA that is advocated and proclaimed at all levels.

There are certain themes and rhetoric that are apparent at all levels of the RCIA and that bear directly on biographical reconstruction. A summary of the way the RCIA is presented throughout the various levels of the RCIA structure is found in a local parish bulletin. Parish bulletins are as Catholic as the pope. Each Sunday parishioners receive a bulletin that details the activities of a parish. The following announcement was found in one such bulletin:

> The Rite of Christian Initiation of Adults is one of the most significant legacies of the Second Vatican Council. It is, in brief, the process, journey in faith by which we initiate new members into the Catholic Church. Conversion is at the heart of this process, consequently, it involves more than passing on knowledge. It involves as well faith and community sharing, reflection on experience and Gospel values. It is a way of being Church.

In this bulletin announcement, the RCIA is described as a journey, a process, a moment in the ongoing conversion of individuals, a manifestation of storytelling and a communal event. Each image was evident throughout the levels and stages of the process of initiation.

RCIA as a Journey

First, the RCIA is described as a journey. On a visit to a parish on the first night of RCIA, evidence of the notion of journey was everywhere. A table with color-coded name tags awaited people. Name tags were coded by where people were "on the journey." Yellow name tags were for the team. Team members also had rainbow-colored stickers in such shapes as butterflies, cats, and rainbows. Other colors represented sponsors, catechumens, and people who just showed up that night. A week later the newly baptized were welcomed back to these meetings. They had the most elaborate name tags of all with gold, black, and red printing and a picture of the church. The newly baptized who also joined the team wore the yellow side showing, thus indicating the primacy of the team, but on the reverse side had elaborate tags reserved for the newly baptized.

The podium at the front of the classroom had a banner hanging from it with the image of a road leading to a cross. The banner read: "Journey Together in Faith, RCIA." At the side of the podium was what was called "the environmental table." This table was supposed to capture the theme for the day. The leader explained that the images on the table represented a journey to salvation. There was a sandy path with rocks leading to salvation. Salvation was represented by the word of God in a Bible. There was a statue of a man placed at the farthest end of the path. The opening song for the night was "Come and Journey with Me." The words of the song, in part, are, "Take the time to look around and love, just love, and walk with each other; come and journey with me."

As chapter 3 will point out, many people I interviewed were attracted to the idea that the RCIA allows people to express their questions. At the RCIA training session this appealing aspect of the process was directly addressed. The speaker said that the job of the RCIA directors was to help people to walk on a journey, and to bring people into the Roman Catholic tradition. Required in this process is providing people with Catholic teaching. People are ready for this when they start asking questions about the church. The speaker summarized: "That is why we operate so much from their questions." Thus, the workshop participants were told that because people were on a journey, they would have questions to which RCIA team members must respond.

The linking of the notion of a journey with biographical reconstruction is evident in the following prayer read at a retreat day for those preparing to be accepted as catechumens. The prayer speaks of the weakness of the past and a desire to see oneself "more clearly than I have before." Defining the past as distinct from the present, and perceiving life in a new way are two hallmarks of biographical reconstruction.

> Lord, you know how weak I have been in the past. Slowly, I understand that it is in my weaknesses that others are able to touch me with your love and bring me life. Thank you, Lord, for creating me to be who I am. Today, Lord, help me not to be overwhelmed by my frailties. Lord, when I started this journey the path was very dark. Help me to see you, and myself, more clearly than I have before.

During this retreat day another image was used that gave implicit approval for biographical reconstruction. The seven participants sat in a circle. The leader passed out some Silly Putty. Each member was to mold the putty into whatever that individual wanted. While the member with the putty molded, the rest of the group was to pray for that person. Implied is the notion that the participants could remold their lives. By inviting the rest of the group to pray for each person while the person remolded, the social nature of the reconstruction was made explicit.

RCIA as a Process

Second, RCIA is described as a process. At a training session for RCIA directors the notion of process was emphasized. The coordinator for the diocese explained that the RCIA is not about programs. "Do not program my life," she said. Emphasizing stages of development and faith she said, "Be with me as I grow into that in my life process." She concluded, "We are about peoples' processes." The speaker for the day addressed adult development. The image she used was that of a weaver. The weaver represents the process of evolving life.

The emphasis on process would seem not to encourage biographical reconstruction. The focus is much more on evolutionary moments than revolutionary moments. Growth and progress are emphasized. A radical break with the past is not emphasized by the concept of process.

RCIA as Religious Conversion

Third, the RCIA and religious conversion are linked. One of the rites in the RCIA is called the "Rite of Calling the Candidates to Continuing Conversion." Conversion is presented as an ongoing and daily reality. Conversion is both evolutionary and revolutionary. RCIA directors were told to "nudge" people along the evolutionary conversion process. They were to encourage conversion in the catechumenate and to share their own conversions. A bishop told a gathering of RCIA team members that the first phase of the RCIA allows the person to come to faith. He said this is an initial conversion into a loving community.

A definitive vision of conversion is presented. First, conversion is experienced by the individual as searching. Next, as a catechumen, the individual is expected to experience conversion as a transformation of morals and mind. Finally, conversion is experienced as religious when the individual is "elected" to be a member of the community. Parker states, "Religious conversion, in short, is the experience of conversion as election" (Parker, 1981:223). We can conclude from Parker's words that without the community that elects there is no *religious* conversion. The distinction between conversion and membership is often blurred in the process. In the RCIA, religious conversion *must* be a social experience. The social emphasis on conversion is such that Dunning writes, "The conversion of catechumens will be individualistic and elitist unless these men and women can be integrated into a community that sees conversion as a *continual* journey constituting the life and mission of the Church" (1981a:340).

RCIA directors were urged to keep the RCIA only for those to whom it was directed. If people have had Catholic education but have not received the sacraments, they do not belong. RCIA is not about faith enrichment or Christian education. The RCIA team members were told that if you let people in who do not belong, then you may lose the real purpose of RCIA and the dimension of conversion journey. The RCIA coordinator for a diocese wrote in a letter to all Directors of Christian Initiation: "As initiation ministers, one of our greatest challenges is to keep the focus on the conversion process as an individual journey of faith which 'takes as long as it takes' for each person."[1]

Finally, the liturgical celebrations are presented as the source of the catechumens' and the parish's conversion. In the words of an RCIA speaker, "The rites convert, they convert us all." The emphasis on conversion not only gives the participants permission to engage in biographical reconstruction, it also requires it. For RCIA teams, the presence or absence of claims or signs of religious conversion among the participants is seen as "a litmus test of authentic faith" (O'Rourke, 1989:21).

The *Rite of Christian Initiation of Adults* is a book which includes both the rubrics for celebrating liturgies in the RCIA, and rules and regulations for each moment in the process. The section "Acceptance into the Order of Catechumens" discusses the prerequisite for making the first step in the RCIA process:

> There must be evidence of the first faith that was conceived during the period of evangelization and precatechumenate and of an initial conversion and intention to change their lives and to enter into a relationship with God in Christ (*Rite of Christian Initiation of Adults: Study Edition*, 1988:19).

Biographical reconstruction is implied and endorsed in the expectation that those who wish to be Catholics intend "to change their lives." Yet, unlike many new religious movements, Roman Catholicism does not require or encourage a public renunciation of one's past. The change of life sought in Catholicism is more subtle and implicit.

RCIA as Storytelling

Fourth, storytelling is part of the process. RCIA directors were told to put a big emphasis on stories of the Catholic tradition at all stages in the process. Storytelling is presented as the way individuals make meaning throughout life. The life review is mentioned by name as a valuable tool in the RCIA (Dunning, 1981b:194). If people join the Catholic religion, they are taking on the stories of the community. The rite of acceptance is about three things, RCIA team members were told: hospitality, trust, and the catechumen's stories. A handbook on implementing the RCIA in parishes states, "The sharing of one's story in light of the scriptures is a major feature of the catechumenate, and…the precatechumenate sets the stage for further story sharing" (Anderson, 1986:24). A Catholic bulletin announcement reads, "The Rite of Christian Initiation of Adults (RCIA) is a process of story sharing which allows those who wish to join our Catholic family to share their own experiences with us, and which offers them an opportunity to hear the story of our faith" (Anderson, 1986:74).

The emphasis on storytelling is meant to be anti-cultural. Dunning says, "The language of story and myth often falls on deaf ears in

America" (1981a:234). American culture "systematically drills us to think in abstractions, not in story-form" (Dunning, 1981a:234). Thus the telling and retelling of one's life story, which is essential in biographical reconstruction, and which American society denies, is incorporated in the RCIA process.

RCIA as a Communal Process

Fifth, the communal nature of the RCIA is constantly emphasized. Berger and Luckmann maintain that a religious community is required to provide a plausibility structure for an individual's conversion (1967:158). The linking of conversion and community in the RCIA process maintains the plausibility of conversion, joining, and the social nature of biographical reconstruction.

The Rite is cited often in claiming that the baptism of new members is the responsibility of the entire community. A pastor's welcoming remarks to a new RCIA class dramatically demonstrates the social binding that those involved in RCIA envision. My field notes are not verbatim quotes from the pastor, but capture the essence of his message and some of his wording:

> There is a spirit of community that grows and develops when people depend on one another and call on the Lord to join. You have to be willing to make yourself dependent. This is not a weakness. The decision to depend is one of great strength. You need to do this to enter into a relationship. With independence comes loneliness. You need to make the decision to allow the sense of community. You need to decide to be dependent. Sharing results in trusting and dependency. The whole staff, especially the priests, want to be part of your journey. You are most welcomed, most loved. We need you. We are depending on you.

At the RCIA director's training session the speaker encouraged the participants to never forget that "our middle name is 'Welcome.'" At a parish RCIA session the director announced a picnic with spouses and family members to "help us bond." At the RCIA team day the workshop participants were told, "Next to God, the reason we are there is people." And, "If we neglect them, we will lose them."

At a seminary class on catechesis, with primary emphasis on the RCIA, future priests were taught that catechesis (thus RCIA) is for the community, not for individuals. Catechesis was described in this class as becoming a member of the community and "a process of coming to conversion." The teaching the seminarians received emphasized the biographical and social nature of catechesis. Catechesis involves a "shared praxis" whereby the catechist shares his/her experience, shares the Christian vision with others, and brings the Christian vision into dialogue with the present experience of those being catechized.

The communal emphasis of the RCIA process results in a social setting where biographical reconstruction is expected to occur. There are some conflicting notions, particularly the notion of process. Yet, when all aspects are considered, a setting is present where the social reconstruction of biography can occur.[2]

These five themes are presented and concretized in training materials used by RCIA leaders. For example, *RCIA Starter Stories* is a two-volume video RCIA tool produced by Liguori Publications (1991). Twenty-four stories are told regarding twenty-four themes (for example, God, temptation, guilt, love, family). One man in his mid-fifties tells of his atheistic youth. He came to know God and Jesus Christ, he says. He then joined the church because, "I had a very positive reservoir of feeling toward the church." Laughing heartily, he states, "If somehow the 'I' of fifteen, twenty years ago could be listening to me now he'd be appalled." This statement is an endorsement of the notion of biographical reconstruction regarding a radical change with the pre-conversion past. His journey of conversion through the community of faith is detailed.

There are, then, strong indications of a social foundation for biographical reconstruction at all levels of the RCIA process. The RCIA is nothing less than a massive social structure formed, knowingly or unknowingly, as a means in which biographical reconstruction can be socially articulated and shared. The subjective reality of biographical reconstruction stands in relation to the objective realities of images of process, journey, storytelling, conversion, and community that are socially defined. As one woman said, "That's one of the reasons we share these things [life stories]; it's to see what we have to change."

One of the attractions of reconstructing one's biography in the RCIA process is that one does so in a built-in, socially shared universe of meaning. As we shall discover in the remainder of this chapter, despite the strong social basis biographical reconstruction is not universally upheld among the older new Catholics I interviewed. Other motivating factors for conversion and membership switching are evident.

BIOGRAPHICAL RECONSTRUCTION REVISITED

As older people told their stories of coming to Roman Catholicism, biographical reconstruction was evident in most, but not all stories. Since Snow and Machalek (1983:269) and Snow and Phillips (1980:431) suggest that converts engage in biographical reconstruction in an intensified and amplified way, the phenomenon should be clearly evident in new Catholics who have experienced religious conversion. Yet, among the people I interviewed, only six individuals indicated clear and unmistakable biographical reconstruction, redefining their life stories *in toto* as Berger and Luckmann (1967) suggest. Sixteen others indicated biographical reconstruction but only in a secondary way. For example, an individual may have spoken about a break with the past but also talked about consistency in values, attitudes or personal history. The total and undeniable aspect of the reconstruction was not present. Five other people demonstrated no clear evidence of biographical reconstruction. The woman who, just three weeks before our interview, inquired about membership in the Catholic Church appeared to be in the midst of biographical reconstruction.

The numbers of individuals who fall into each category are given only to put the stories in context. Far more important are the ways in which biographical reconstruction was present, or absent, in stories of religious conversion and/or denominational membership switching. The following sections tell the story of biographical reconstruction and religious conversion.

BIOGRAPHICAL RECONSTRUCTION CLEARLY EVIDENT

The question that most directly explores biographical reconstruction asks if, since going through the RCIA and becoming Catholic, the new Catholic feels more like two people or the same person. Presumably by indicating one feels like two people the radical break with the past that biographical reconstruction of converts includes would be at least possible in the individual's view of his/her past.

All six individuals who strongly indicated biographical reconstruction, and who said they had a religious conversion, also indicated they felt more like two people. For example, one woman spoke about a monastic retreat: "So I flew over there and was at [the name of the monastery] for a week. I came back a different person." Throughout our interview she spoke of the dramatic change in her life since beginning her efforts to become Catholic.

A typical exchange in this category was with Dave, a sixty-one-year-old man who waited to become a Catholic until his wife would join him. He exuded enthusiasm. His personality was pleasant. His eyes were engaging. During our interview he literally sat on the edge of his couch. With his arms and legs moving for emphasis, he was a man fully engaged in our discussion:

> *Some people, when they go through the RCIA to become Catholic, they describe themselves as almost two persons: the person they were before Catholic and the person they are now.*
>
> Oh, yeah. Yeah, I never heard that one, but I'll sign up for that one.
>
> *As opposed, say, I feel pretty much like the same person.*
>
> Oh, no, you're an entirely different person, the way you act, the way you treat people—You stop and think. That's what it is: you stop others and you think, and you didn't stop before. But you stop and say, "Wait a minute! I'm a new me! I'm supposed to, y'know, stop." Did I say, "I'm eating; did I say grace?" I didn't thank God because of this food, and this is God's food, not mine." Oh, it's a whole—Yeah, it's a whole new human being! No question about that.

Dave's description of himself as "a whole new human being" clearly indicates a radical break with his pre-Catholic biography. The entire interview was biographical reconstruction in action. Dave indicates a "then I thought, but now I know" (Berger and Luckmann, 1967:160) pattern in talking about his feeling of destiny in becoming a Catholic:

> I used to drive by there and would not be able to not look at that church and appreciate how beautiful that church was. That church was destined to be something to me and I think I knew it. Okay?

> That sounds maybe—[loony whistle] way out there—[chuckle] but that's a feeling I had, and I had no desire to go and knock on anybody's door or anything like that, but I did, didn't I?

Dave's break with his pre-Catholic biography is also evident in his answer to the question, "What have been the most important events or moments in your life?"

> Truthfully, all of 'em since RCIA. Truthfully. I mean, that forgoes the fact that I, y'know, got married. That wasn't the greatest event in my life; the birth of my children were—but not really, not down—in—here [pointing to his heart]. My first communion and my baptism was a great highlight to me; I've a sense of accomplishment more satisfying than anything I've done in my life.

In this paragraph Dave indicates that all in his past biography, including his marriage and children, is now redefined in light of his membership in the church. Dave's comments link the notion of biographical reconstruction with the embracing of a master role (Snow and Machalek, 1983). All other roles and perspectives are secondary to the role and perspective of being a convert. In Berger and Luckmann's terms, Dave has internalized the convert role (1967:74). His role as a convert has become subjectively meaningful for him and a prism in which to discover all other personal and social meaning.

Notice as well that Dave gives prominence to "the RCIA." He does not say events in his life have been important "since becoming Catholic" or "since my conversion." Rather, "the RCIA" is the important notion and defining break with the past.

Finally, Dave indicates an active engagement in the life review. Two significant issues of death emerged in our interview. First, Dave recalled childhood memories surrounding the death of his great-grandmother. At age fifteen he recalled "the blackest hour of my early life" as he prayed that God would save his great-grandmother from death. Later, he recalled the recent death of his mother. His wife found his mother dead in bed.

> And she found her dead in the bedroom. After the initial shock of that, of course, I went back in with her and knelt to pray. I don't recall much about the prayer, but I remember something told me to look at my mother and she wasn't there anymore; I looked at

her—she wasn't there anymore, Father. Something said, "You don't have anything to worry about. Your mother's with God." And that was it, and that is it right now. I haven't had—The tears went away and everything was fine. And that was the biggest revelation. Since then, I think it's been a constant thing for me to not avoid—growing and getting away from one of the great fears I had all during my childhood was death: I was afraid of death.

As our interview progressed we continued to discuss issues of death. Dave said he had a lifelong fear of death that he had finally overcome. He was particularly attracted to the parish where he enrolled in the RCIA after attending a funeral at the church. Dave then started to relate his memories of death to his joining the church. He said, "Suddenly I just realized that a lot of things have evolved with death with me in the church, hasn't it?" Dave then suggested one of the purposes of our interview may have been to help him face issues of death. "I now see something I've never seen before: My road to Catholicism is through a pattern of the fear of death, and I think maybe that's God's way of rewarding me, huh? Perhaps; I don't know."

Dave demonstrates two of Butler's suggestions regarding the life review: it often focuses on issues of death and is often accomplished on an unconscious level. As Dave summarized, "There's some other things maybe I should've said in background that I just wasn't remembering." Dave's story also links the life review with biographical reconstruction. He deals with the issues of death in his life through the life review, and then with the newly acquired framework of Roman Catholicism, he reconstructs the events leading up to and finding their fulfillment in his joining the Catholic Church through the RCIA.

The religious nature of Dave's life review and biographical reconstruction is indicated in his words, "I know that I'm going to look back, and be more comfortable as far as a lot of things in my life because I'm more mature. There was a lot of change in my thinking between fifty and sixty years of age, okay? And it's comfortable. And I believe that God makes that happen to us...." Dave said he could not separate what is maturity and what is "God's gift." For him, they were one and the same.

After our interview Dave told his wife we had talked about something he had not thought of, or knew, that he would share with her later. Referring to his discovery about death, he said it was "something I know that I didn't know I knew."

The interview with Dave was a lesson in biographical reconstruction and the importance of the convert role in an individual's life. Two years after his acceptance into the Catholic Church he was still reconstructing his biography in light of his role as a convert.

Edna is a sixty-seven-year-old housewife. She personifies independence. On the day of our interview she had just returned from one of her frequent trips to the local library. She was wearing tennis sneakers and an autographed tennis visor. Her hair style seemed to indicate her general approach to life; it was functionally cut and simply combed to one side. She wore two crosses, a gold cross on a chain and a red cross on her collar. Edna's answer to "the most important events in your life" question echoes the same themes as Dave's answer:

> Well, the finding out that I was adopted, the moment that I found out that I was a National Honor student—that was a great reward after working hard in high school. Then, when I got the radio program—that was a big moment, and then when, of course, when I got married, and...then I have to say, but of all of those—I guess it's because it's—maybe because it's the most recent and it's changed—it has enhanced my life to such an extent in every direction and stretching out, my joining the Catholic Church; really, I feel like a different person; I really—I'm sorry that I'm old—I told that to Father Paul. I really wish I were young because this has opened up so many different channels that I didn't know were there that I would like to be able to continue on. Maybe I can when I get to the next life or something, but I would like to— Y'know, I really wish that I had—this had happened when I was little.

Once again, Edna's story gives support to the biographical reconstruction thesis. She directly attributes the change in her life to joining the Catholic Church. Everything else is secondary. Her biographical reconstruction is such that she wishes she could reconstruct her life even further by introducing Roman Catholicism in her life when she was "little."

Note that Edna, similar to Dave, attributes the change in her life to "my joining the church" and not to her religious conversion. For many people I interviewed the two events could not be separated. Edna spoke of her religious conversion as a gradual process over a period of a few months in which she felt a "tremendous enlightenment and was kind of lifted up out of myself." The time to which Edna attributed a religious conversion was "right away after I was confirmed." I asked her, "Which would you say has been more important in your life, becoming Catholic or that conversion experience?" Her response indicated the linking of the two events:

> Well, I guess becoming a Catholic is the slightly more, yes, because that—in that I recognized that the conversion is one thing—you're given that as a kind—as a gift, but then—but then you must be responsible and develop that gift, with God's help, to the best of your ability, so being a Catholic would be the best way, in my opinion, to—My feeling about it is that that would be the best possible opportunity to—to develop it.

The change in the lives of the six people who engaged clearly in biographical reconstruction is reflected not only in feeling like a different person, but also in attitudes, outlooks and behaviors. For example, a sixty-three-year-old man answered the question, "Is there anything that frightens you about the future?" with the response, "There was before I was baptized. I was afraid of death, but now I'm not anymore."

A sixty-five-year-old professional musician addressed the question, "Have your beliefs or values changed over time?"

> Well, I guess the first twenty to twenty-five years that I was married it was a very materialistic philosophy of life. It was really enjoying the good life, quote quote, you know. Which meant having everything. So I was really after buying things, looking forward to traveling, all very materialistic goals, really. People were not all that important to me. I didn't realize it at the time, but in retrospect I can look back now and see that people relationships outside of just the immediate family were not that high a priority for me.

This response is framed in exemplary biographical reconstruction language: "I didn't realize it at the time, but in retrospect I can look back now and see...." This statement is also evidence of an active engagement in the life review.

In response to the same question regarding change in values or beliefs, Dave replied, "Oh yeah. Oh, tremendously since Catholicism entered my life." Even though this question was posed before discussing each person's change to Catholicism, a change in values or beliefs is not surprising, given the fact that each person has changed religious affiliation, which entails changes in institutional belief. Later in the interview each person was asked a more generic question about a personal change in life relating to changes in "personal attitudes or outlook." The question also more directly addressed any connection with becoming Catholic: "Has there been any change in your personal outlook or attitude toward life as a result of becoming Catholic?"

Each of the six persons in this category cited significant change. Two people mentioned being happier, three people mentioned a change in temperament. One person mentioned being much stronger on issues such as abortion and euthanasia.

Ben, a sixty-three-year-old man who spent most of his life working at hard labor, captures the essence of the six responses in this category, and does so in a way that clearly shows the effects of biographical reconstruction:

> But they talk about me in the neighborhood, y'know, about years back; I'd be out in the garage, start drinking beer come hell and high water, and we hashed religion, we hashed everything out, out there, and I joined the Catholic religion and become baptized and I calmed down—y'know. I used to be a rowdy dude. I thought I knew so much about everything; I never knew nothing. That's the way we were out here.

Ben describes his pre-Catholic biography as being a different character, one who "used to be a rowdy dude" and "thought I knew so much about everything." The extreme dichotomy that Ben presents is indicative of his complete engagement in biographical reconstruction: "My old life is forgotten and gone; let sleepin' dogs lie. I'm living for the future now."[3]

Ben also implies a social nature to his reconstruction, saying, "That's the way *we* were out here." His personal change has had implications, in his view, on the neighborhood. The social nature of Ben's reconstruction within the RCIA process is addressed. By sharing life stories, Ben said, "You can talk outward; you can say it, y'know: 'Hey, this is what I *was* and this is what I am now and this is where I'm gonna be.'" Ben's narrative exemplifies the break from the past that biographical reconstruction describes, the linking of the three modes of time that the life review describes, and the social nature of the process that this book describes.

A final example of the undeniable presence of biographical reconstruction comes from a seventy-nine-year-old man who claimed that his experience in the RCIA and becoming Catholic was a religious conversion. He stated, "I was baptized and I recognized it as being baptized in the church and my belief and everything. It has definitely changed since that night very, very much." The reconstruction that he directly relates to religious conversion and baptism is evident in his answer to the question, "How would you say that your experience differs from that of a lifelong Catholic?"

> At the present time, I don't think there's that much difference between my life and a lifelong Catholic. I'm throwing out the years before this, now; I'm just throwing those out—completely out the window. I'm not even—They aren't even—They never come into my mind anymore.

To summarize, all six people who unmistakably spoke of their past as radically separated from the present also indicated they had had a religious conversion.[4] Even though "religious conversion" is an ambiguous term at best, the unanimously affirmative perception of religious conversion in this group is significant to note. Their personal narratives are vibrant accounts of dramatic change in their biographies as a result of becoming Catholic. The experience of the individuals in this group supports the research that links religious conversion and biographical reconstruction.

BIOGRAPHICAL RECONSTRUCTION NOT STRONGLY INDICATED

Sixteen people were placed in this category based on statements in our interviews which both affirmed and denied biographical reconstruction and/or affirmed biographical reconstruction but also indicated considerable consistency in personal stories. The hallmark of biographical reconstruction, a striking break with one's past, was not present in any of the life stories told by these people.[5]

No one in this group described her/himself as feeling like two persons. Although many did speak of change in their lives, they spoke of change coupled with personal consistency. For example, one woman suggested, "I feel pretty much like the same person, except for more complete." Another responded, "Well, my whole personality hasn't changed, actually. My beliefs changed, my drive for doing things has increased...." Finally, like a number of people in this category, June related her feeling of consistency with the fact that she has attended church with her husband and family for many years:

> I think I am pretty much the same person, but I think I'm more, at least because, don't forget, I went to that church for almost forty years without joining, and I think I'm pretty much the same person except now I feel, I feel at peace with it. I made up my mind and I like what I did.

Larry, as well, related his consistent participation in Catholicism over many decades to the lack of dramatic change in his life:

> But for me I was always there and the big change was just coming into it officially, which was a big thing for me. I don't want to belittle it certainly, a very important step and a very exciting step, and my life has changed as a result of that. But I don't feel it was as dramatic a step as if I had not been going to church over the years.

Despite such consistency in personal narrative, some indication of biographical reconstruction was present in the stories of each of the sixteen people in this category.

Cathy, a sixty-three-year-old woman who exudes energy, spoke about her life as if she were wrapping up a nice package. Throughout her life she had felt an attraction to the Catholic Church. As a child she would go to church occasionally with her cousins. As an adult, especially when facing difficult times, she would stop at a Catholic church near her apartment to pray. When asked, "What has given your life meaning?" Cathy spoke about "my own kind of faith." She then told the story of grappling with the sudden death of a friend's teenage son:

> And it took me a long time to accept Mark's death. But I fully believe Mark was blessed. God sent him here for a purpose, and

Stories of Biographical Reconstruction

he was finished so God took him. It took me a long time to come to that point though. I mean a long time in my life to be able to truthfully say that I understand that, that God sent Mark down here for a purpose; his purpose was finished and he took him back [said in a matter of fact tone]. I can accept it now; a few years ago I could not have done that.

What's the difference between then and now?

RCIA has made a big difference in my life.[6]

The next question I asked was, "Have your beliefs changed over time?" She answered, "Very much so since I have been in RCIA." Thus Cathy compares her ability to accept Mark's death to an inability she would have had "a few years ago." Notice that, similar to Dave, Cathy attributes the change in her life to *the RCIA*, not the Catholic Church.[7]

During our interview, there were other clear signs of biographical reconstruction. When asked if there had been any change in her personal outlooks or attitudes toward life since becoming Catholic, Cathy responded, "Everything. I am a happier person. I am more outgoing. I have a lot more faith." In describing her baptism Cathy stated, "It was like at that baptism something took over my life."

Yet, in describing her friends' reactions, Cathy said, "All my friends thought I was crazy. They kept telling me, 'My God, here you are in your late fifties and what are you trying to prove by becoming Catholic?' In fact, it finally got to the point where I said to them, 'Either you will accept me—I mean, I was no different, I still went out with them.'" Cathy concluded her story of her friends' reaction: "I told 'em…I'm not going to be any different. I'm not going to preach to you. I am not going to do anything to change our relationship. But I feel very strongly that I have to do this." Cathy's categorizations of herself as "I was no different" and "I'm not going to be any different" are examples of indicators contrary to a strong biographical reconstruction.[8]

A final example from Cathy's interview emphasizes the often contradictory indicators of biographical reconstruction in this group:

Have you dealt with your memories, or have you dealt with your life differently since becoming Catholic?

> Much more so; I am much more aware of God being there and how you know you can be kind to people, and you can care about people whereas before, I'll be very truthful, I can be very nasty.

Cathy's last statement captures the dichotomy: "Whereas before...I can be very nasty." Notice Cathy did not say, "I used to be very nasty." Rather, she spoke in the present tense of a disposition that is linked to her past. Typical statements of biographical reconstruction would be, "The old me used to be very nasty," or "Before becoming Catholic I was very nasty."

Another example of both affirmation and denial of biographical reconstruction is found in Sally's story. Sally is sixty-four years old and has retired from a career as a professional cartoonist. Her work on various well-known animated television programs was reflected in the colorful and art-filled decor of her home. When asked, "What does it mean now for you to be Catholic?" she responded, "It means everything, I guess. New meaning to life and a new way of thinking." But she described herself in these words: "I think I'm the same person really," and "As I've gotten older, I feel that my feelings haven't changed that much through the years." Sally's framework is a departmentalized biographical reconstruction. She changed chapters of her life, but not the whole story. She described a new way of thinking but described her life story, her values, and her feelings as being consistent.

Deb, a sixty-one-year-old operations manager, did not strongly indicate a religious conversion in her life, but did suggest that the change in membership itself may have prompted a deeper engagement in the life-review process and biographical reconstruction:

> *Do you find yourself looking back much in your life?*
>
> I probably have more in the last three or four years because of this and been more introspective, I think, because of this, and normally, no, no, I don't.
>
> *Do you think that looking back at your life or dealing with memories had anything to do with your becoming Catholic?*
>
> Probably, probably, but, not so much looking back; it's just something that I've always felt, that it was something that I should have done years ago. I've always felt that there was a mistake

made when I didn't become Catholic before we were married; I think if I had, it might have been a chance to actually preserve or build or do a better job with that.

Deb's final statement is an allusion to her decision earlier in life not to become Catholic, and her failed marriage. By becoming Catholic now, she suggests, she is correcting (reconstructing) the mistakes of her past.

Given the lack of dramatic or total break with the past, the people in this category showed far more engagement in the life-review process than they did in biographical reconstruction. Maureen, for example, a sixty-one-year-old woman who had changed from very little religious activity in her life to being an RCIA activist, stated:

> One of the hard things at night trying to go to sleep is going back over the mistakes of a lifetime, yet, but, if I didn't do all those things I wouldn't be here, would I? Yeah, I am hard on myself; I don't want to be back there, I don't want to be twenty again. I like being sixty-one. I don't want to be twenty again. Although it's a little bit scary for me knowing that, you know, I'm a senior citizen now. That's a little surprising. You look in the mirror and say, "Where did the girl go?"

Mirror gazing is a manifestation of the life review. Looking in the mirror is a means of introspection. Maureen also links her life review to the fact she is now a senior citizen.

The challenge to the biographical reconstruction thesis comes, not from the prominence of the life review, but from those people who identified religious conversion in their life, yet did not clearly and strongly indicate biographical reconstruction. This fact seriously challenges the notion that biographical reconstruction is accomplished on an intensified level in those experiencing religious conversion, yet the fact is each of these eight individuals did show some indication of biographical reconstruction. Still, biographical reconstruction literature does place much weight on the intensified nature of a convert's reconstruction. The experience of these older new Catholics suggests the need for a nuanced approach to biographical reconstruction. A suggestion for future research would be a comparison of Catholic and Protestant individuals who claim to have had a religious conversion. What influence do the differing emphases on an immediate and identifiable conversion (Protestant) and gradual and daily conversion (Catholic) have on an individual's biographical reconstruction?

BIOGRAPHICAL RECONSTRUCTION NOT EVIDENT

This third category is marked by individuals who speak of consistency in their life stories without any clear indication of biographical reconstruction. One man's statement captures this attitude: "I'm a firm believer that…we are who we are this day and we're continually, continually evolving and growing, even at my age. And, y'know, I'm trying to think of some of the ways that I've, that I've changed." Fred concluded that perhaps he was more broadminded and less judgmental than he was before becoming Catholic, but his story is one of "continually evolving and growing" and not one of radical change.

John is an example of an individual who not only indicates consistency in his life story but also explicitly denies "a big change." John, who is Sally's husband, became Catholic five years after she did. While Sally was somewhat reserved during our interview, John was engaged. Sally sat straight up on the couch answering quickly and directly the questions posed. John was far more relaxed. The way the couple dressed was indicative of their approach. Sally wore a coordinated pant suit. John wore shorts and a Dodger tee shirt. I asked John:

> *Have you found your personal attitudes or outlooks changed at all since you have become Catholic?*
>
> [pause] I—That's a hard one for me to judge. I don't know if I'm quite good at introspection. I don't see a big change. How's that—I mean, it's not a major thing; I don't see anything major here. We go to our church on Sunday quite religiously if we are feeling well. I don't think that there's been a big change in my life. There's been no change in my attitudes towards people and my family or friends to speak of.

A key event in John and Sally's life was the sudden death of their son. Without any previous indication, their son collapsed one morning and died from meningitis. John's reflections on his son's death indicate this event is still very much part of his ongoing biography:

At nine o'clock I got up, and I didn't see him in bed and went out and his car was locked. I went back in and he rolled off the bed. And he was dead. He was still warm. I got the ambulance. He was dead on arrival. And after I found out—I mean, my doctor, he delivered my two children and also my grandchildren, someone we've known all these years, he told me, he says, "There are strains of meningitis; there are all kinds of viruses. There is some strain of meningitis that when they vomit they die within about an hour." And he said, "If I could have had him at that point, even if I knew exactly what it was, I could not have saved him." He said, "Shots of sulfur in the spine are the only thing that I could do." And he said. "When they vomit it doesn't work." He said, "There are some strains that are so fast-acting that once they vomit they are gone in about an hour." And that's just about what happened to him. He tried to relieve me of my—why didn't I do this, or do that? These are the things that go through your mind. When anything happens, even though you personally couldn't resolve it—I didn't have the responsibility—you go through this mental anguish of trying to see what could I have done, what should I have done.

Recreating your steps.

And this is the parental problem of, and of course…. If you should have done something and didn't, you understand it would even be worse. I mean this type of problem. You know with my kid it was much more specific, but nevertheless you can't keep from regurgitating these mental anguishes. It takes forever to get through. It took years to pound it out slowly. It's twenty-five years now almost. And still it's very strong.

Here John indicates the life review is powerfully active in his life. What people often regret in the life review is not so much what they did in life but what they did not do. John puts this notion into specific words. If John had engaged in biographical reconstruction, he might say instead, "At the time, and in the years following, I anguished over what I might have been able to do to save my son, but now I realize it was not my fault; there was nothing I could have done. Now that anguish is gone." John is actively engaged in life review and not engaged in biographical reconstruction.

John and Sally were interviewed separately. The ways they

addressed their son's death indicate diverse approaches to biographical reconstruction. Sally mentioned her son's death twice in our interview. When I asked her, "If you had to live your life over again would there be things you would do differently?" she responded, "Well, I suppose John mentioned that we lost our son. If I knew that was going to happen, well, of course we would have done something about that, but other than that I lived a good life." When asked, "What has been the worst part of your life?" she responded, "Losing our son. It was very hard." Sally's responses differed in tone and intensity when compared to John's responses. Unlike her husband, their son's death was not a prominent issue in our interview. Sally seemed to have compartmentalized that experience in her biography. "Other than that" her life has been good. John, on the other hand, found the death of his son still a "very strong" force.

The people in this category do not challenge the biographical reconstruction thesis insofar as all five individuals indicated they did not have what they would describe as a religious conversion. However, Snow and Phillips' (1980) research does not draw a distinction between *membership* in the Shoshu Buddhist Movement and personal *religious conversion*. Their sample population, similar to the sample population in this study, is new members. The authors do not distinguish between those who claim religious conversion and those who do not. The authors write, "We thus assume that the population from which the sample was drawn consists primarily of 'core converts' or 'true believers'" (1980:433). In their presentation of the data they never state that the people in their study clearly indicated a religious conversion. Thus we assume Snow and Phillips are primarily testing the influence of new membership, not religious conversion. Snow and Phillips claim that all new members in their study indicated biographical reconstruction. Our study suggests all new members do not indicate biographical reconstruction.

BIOGRAPHICAL RECONSTRUCTION IN PROCESS

Only one individual indicated biographical reconstruction in process. Yet the experience of this woman is instructive of the ways in which biographical reconstruction may prompt denominational joining or religious conversion.

I met Lula the night before our interview at a parish RCIA

session. She had begun inquiry into the Catholic Church three weeks before our interview. When I asked her for an interview, she was obliging but found it difficult to believe there was anything in her story worth telling. She runs her own business so we agreed to meet at the parish rectory early the next morning before she went to work.

Promptly at eight she arrived in her Continental automobile. During our interview she was somewhat of a contradiction. She was both shy and revealing. She addressed each question thoroughly and thoughtfully. The many pieces of her life, such as past and present, and work and family, were carefully sorted out and presented in her story.

Prominent in her story were her mother and her daughter. Her mother suffered a stroke five years ago which left her paralyzed and unable to speak. Lula, her daughter, and a private physician take care of her mother. Lula and her mother often talked about the need to be baptized. They intended some day to be baptized. Lula's daughter became Catholic after marrying a Catholic.

Lula's own decision to explore Catholicism clearly indicates life review and biographical reconstruction in process. Speaking about the decision to become Catholic, Lula stated:

> And I've come to the conclusion in my life now that, she's [mother] stabilized to the point that I am not in and out of the hospital quite so much, and I thought it was maybe about time I got my life together.

Significant to notice is the fact that Lula directly relates the decision to become Catholic with getting "my life together." Later in our interview Lula directly related putting her life together with her age:

> And like I say, we didn't take the time. So like I said, so I decided it's time, it's time to get my life together. I'm getting old! [laughing] We don't expect to get old, do you know that?

A few questions later I probed the age connection:

> *Did becoming Catholic when you did have anything to do with your age? You hinted a little bit about that. You said it's—I'm getting old and it's time to put my life in order.*

Well, not really. It's just that I look back and think, how many years have I lost? I don't want to lose any more years. I want to start living, I mean right now, correctly.

In this response Lula indicates a life review by saying, "I look back and think how many years have I lost." She indicates a desire for a new biography by saying she wants "to start living, I mean right now, correctly." Lula indicated in our interview that, in her estimation, she had not lived correctly up until then. She has great esteem, even adulation, for her mother. Almost reverently she named her mother as the person who has had the most impact in her life. When I asked, "What has her impact been?" Lula replied, in part, "She lives in this moment, and she never thinks about what could have been, what should have been, or anything." She concluded, "She's friends with everybody. And so I guess that's why I admire her. And I am not that way, I am sorry to say." Unlike her perception of her mother, Lula obviously considers "what could have been" and "what should have been" in her life story. She does not see such concerns as valuable.

Lula's dilemma is an example of a common trait of the convert as social type as described by Snow and Machalek:

> Gripped by the realization that preconversion interpretations were erroneous, the convert comes to redefine the past "correctly." Old facts and aspects of one's biography are thus given new meanings. Not only are former identities evaluated negatively but the course and character of the convert's life history is typically reconstructed as troublesome, misdirected, even loathsome (Snow and Machalek, 1983:267).

Berger and Luckmann also address the importance of perceiving correctness in one's life:

> The individual passing from one biographical phase to another can view himself as repeating a sequence that is given in the "nature of things," or in his own "nature." That is, he can reassure himself that he is living "correctly." The "correctness" of his life program is thus legitimated on the highest level of generality. As the individual looks back upon his life, his biography is intelligible to him in these terms. As he projects himself into the

future, he may conceive of his biography as unfolding within a universe whose ultimate coordinates are known (1967:99–100).

Lula's experiences exemplify the transitional nature of the life evaluation, the search for "correctness," and the universe whose coordinates are known, which she has found in the Catholic Church. The social nature of Lula's reconstruction is found precisely in the universe of meaning that Roman Catholicism represents for Lula.

Lula does not indicate she has had a religious conversion, but she does directly relate the dynamics of the life review and biographical reconstruction to becoming Catholic. Lula sees the Catholic Church as an agent of change in her life review and reconstruction. She spoke about the sharing of life stories that her RCIA group had been engaged in over the three weeks before our interview. I asked her if she saw any connection between the sharing of life stories and becoming Catholic:

> Other than perhaps maybe it's sharing your story and leaving that behind and turning to the future. Being a Catholic what is past is gone, and you can't do anything about it.

In the following exchange Lula connects her generic impressions of the letting go of the past with her own desire to be Catholic:

> *Do you have any insight into how your experience might differ from a younger convert or younger inquirer?*
>
> Well, the only thing that I can really think of is, I know as you are younger, you might be—you might be joining a church being afraid. I don't think I'm afraid. It's just a matter of, I want to change the way I look. And I want to be—Nobody can sit and say God has forgiven me for all of the things that I have said. Well, maybe if I am connected with a church he might forgive a little bit, a little bit more than if I just asked. And I think sometimes the younger people that get in trouble, and they don't know where to turn, and they are looking for a church, and that was the right place for them.

Thus Lula sees in the church a means to make her "past gone." She seeks movement from the feeling she has of being unforgivable to the prospect for increased forgiveness that the Catholic Church offers, in her estimation.

What makes Lula unique, when compared to all the other individuals interviewed, is that she desires biographical reconstruction but is not yet there. In the quotation immediately above she stated, "I want to change the way I look." Elsewhere in our interview she stated, "I just hope I change and become a little more at home, not so private," and "I'm always sort of worried, and sometimes gentleness doesn't come through when you worry. And I am working on it, very much so. I am not the type of person, I haven't been the type of person, that has temper and everything upset in my life. However, with the push of the last few years, sometimes it is very difficult not to be on the run all the time." In these statements Lula makes clear her desire to change. She seeks the radical break that biographical reconstruction entails. By saying, "I haven't been the type of person..." Lula implies she wishes to change and be the type of person who is gentle. Whereas in some of the other life stories, biographical reconstruction is portrayed as a result of, or indication of, becoming Catholic, for Lula biographical reconstruction is a motivation for becoming Catholic. Her experience indicates that biographical reconstruction may not only be an indicator of religious conversion, but in many instances may also be a motivator for religious seeking.

By presenting the stories of these older Catholics, I have demonstrated that biographical reconstruction has various manifestations in the lives of the participants in this study. An examination of the prayer group offers a comparison of biographical reconstruction being present, or absent, in the stories of veteran Catholics.

THE STORIES OF LIFELONG CATHOLICS

Almost every Monday for four years, six women gathered at St. Anthony's parish to pray. Each Monday, at ten minutes to eleven, the door of a quaintly decorated convent was opened. A seventy-year-old Catholic religious sister would sit and wait for the group to arrive; sometimes the members arrived together, sometimes they arrived alone. Always they greeted each other with a hug. As they walked from the front hall into a warm and cozy chapel they talked about the previous week. They asked each other about their children, or their health, or their bills, or whatever was prominent in their lives the last time they met.

The members of the group are diverse in background. Ellen is a small and determined eighty-six-year-old native of Ireland. For most of her life she has worked as a nanny and traveled throughout the world. During the course of this study Ellen moved to a nursing home in Long Beach. Darleen is another member who had to discontinue going to the meetings because of poor health. She is ninety-two years old. Darleen, and the rest of the members to be described, are widowed mothers. Last year she had a near-fatal heart attack. Paula is a stately woman of eighty-five years. In her seventies she had switched from the Episcopal Church to the Catholic Church. Joan is a small and soft-spoken native of Missouri. She devotes three days a week to volunteering as a Lay Eucharistic Minister and as a preparer of food for the homeless. She is eighty years old. Finally, Karen is a Scotswoman of eighty years. She takes great pride in the work she did as executive housekeeper at a number of nursing homes on the East and West coasts of America.

The prayer group was formed five years ago during the liturgical season of Lent (forty days of preparation for Easter). Sister Agnes was recovering from a bleeding ulcer. She was anxious to get back to work. After consulting with other members of St. Anthony's parish staff, she decided to conduct a scripture study during the Lenten season. Each week about one dozen older women would come together to study the Bible. They would consult with biblical literature and with each other's experience. At the conclusion of the sessions some of the participants asked Sister Agnes if she would continue to meet with the group. Six of the original twelve members continued to meet each Monday.

During the first eighteen months of its existence, the prayer group began changing its focus. Sister Agnes began to encourage the group to discuss how the scriptures they were studying affected their personal lives. Agnes believes the group became more and more comfortable with personal sharing. She said: "And as we went on that is what they wanted rather than preparing the Sunday readings." The group had changed to such an extent that during my four months of observation, scriptures were not explicitly on the agenda. Scriptural references would be made in relationship to personal issues that were being discussed.

The format of the meeting was very predictable. After gathering in a close circle of chairs, and "catching up" with each other, Agnes asked each member what her week had been like. Each member discussed important issues in her life: the illness of a son, the care of a friend, a struggle with anger at God, and the like. Next, Agnes played a meditative song. A few words might be exchanged about the content of the song. Songs were usually categorized as "beautiful" by the members, "Oh, that was beautiful." After the song, Agnes presented some written material to guide reflection. Poems, prayers, and other devotional literature were read slowly and deliberately by Agnes. Pauses after sentences, paragraphs, or stanzas allowed the members the opportunity to verbalize what personal meaning the words had. The discussion was open, with many personal and significant issues discussed. As the meeting continued, Sister Agnes monitored the time. Some of the members attended a 12:10 mass in the nearby church. At about noon Agnes reminded the group of items to keep in prayer during the week: "Let's remember Ellen's trip to Long Beach.". . . "We will keep Karen's son in our prayers." Members committed themselves to one another through prayer, embraced, and headed in their different directions.

St. Anthony's is a large and active parish, which recently celebrated its one-hundred-year anniversary. Currently there are nearly six thousand registered parishioners. The church building is an imposing Spanish structure that rises from a busy street. The attendance at church services is impressive. About four hundred people attend a total of three services each day. Each of the members of the prayer group goes to mass each day. On weekends the church, which holds about one thousand people, is usually full. At some masses there is standing room only.

In 1991, Sister Agnes retired from active ministry. She moved away from the parish and the prayer group, despite promises to reunite each month, disbanded.

In each of the members, and in each of the meetings, the life-review process was evident. Biographical reconstruction was far less evident. A typical meeting demonstrates this point:

Slowly, gently and deliberately Sister Agnes reads a line for meditation. Each word rolls softly off her tongue. Her words are soothing. Her tone and approach are conducive to quiet reflection. She poses the question for the group, and for each member, "What have I done to get to know myself?" She waits and adds, "What means were the most helpful?" Ellen responds first. She says she does not like to spend a lot of time thinking about herself. It is like when a doctor asks when a pain began and when it went away. She once had been a nanny for a couple of boys who were seeing a psychiatrist. The brothers would have to write down everything that happened to them as it happened. Ellen says this was foolish.

Sister Agnes probes Ellen, saying that she seems to know herself well. Ellen says that much wisdom comes in retrospect. It is like two sides of a coin: you do not see the other side until later. There is another pause. The members consider Ellen's offering.

Karen breaks the silence with her own insight. She states that she keeps a daily journal. At the beginning of each day she writes what she hopes to accomplish. At the end of the day she marks off what she has completed. The uncompleted tasks or goals are moved to the next page, to begin the next day's list.

Paula says she gets in touch with herself through her "sense of failure." She remembers all those things that she has not done in life that she intended to do. Ellen encourages Paula not to focus on the things she has not done. Such focusing will prevent Paula from doing what she needs to do that day.

This one excerpt, from the February 26th meeting of the prayer group, demonstrates some essential elements of the life-review process. Ellen appears to be engaging in the life review without recognizing her own activity of reminiscence. At first she proclaims she does not spend a lot of time thinking about herself (and her life), but then she speaks about the wisdom and insight that come in retrospect. Her description of the revelatory nature of life, like the two sides of a coin, suggests Ellen is seeking the integration that Erik Erikson (1968) upheld. Ellen is able to see "both sides" of life and to place these aspects into a unitary picture. Her proclamation of wisdom coming in retrospect, and not seeing "the other side of the coin" until later in life, may be a hint of biographical reconstruction, yet the story she tells is told as a whole.

A journal is a fundamental tool in life-review therapy. Karen's particular use of a journal demonstrates her grounding in the present and her hopes for the future. Through the life review Karen is discovering meaning in the present and hope for the future. Karen's life review includes life preview.

Recall that the life review most often focuses on not what a person did in life but what a person did not do. Paula's "sense of failure" focuses on what she did not do, but intended to do. Ellen, who seems to have resolved this conflict, shares with Paula her insights on how to bring the past in line with "what you need to do today."

The above description is just one moment (about five minutes) in over thirty hours of observations. These manifestations of the life review are even more impressive given the fact that the prayer group was not centered around memory or life review. The group was not formed with a life-review agenda. The structure of the interactions encouraged a constant focus on the present, yet a group negotiation of a life review was evident in every meeting.

Sister Agnes's style of leadership facilitated personal sharing and reflective personal expressions. Her trademark question was, "What about Paula?" or "What about Joan?" As the women of the group discussed the concerns of their lives, they usually talked about friends or family members. Agnes would ask, "Well, what about Karen, how is she?" This probing usually was received with a smile. By this question Agnes demonstrated that she cared. Reflections on the self were encouraged.

Karen's narrative demonstrates the consistency and progress that marked the stories the lifelong Catholics told. Karen said, "I am really still what I was." She stated:

> I am perfectly satisfied with what I am. Really and truly. Now except for the fact that I can't lift this [her arm] and it bugs me a little. I am perfectly satisfied with every stage of my life I went through…it's been good. I think I kept myself so busy that I didn't have time to be sorry for myself. You're just glad to get through each day.…So I can't say I really have any regrets. I can't say there is any period in my life that I can say, "I wish it didn't happen." I think from everything that happened to me I gained strength.

Another example comes from Darleen. One of the most traumatic moments in her life was her husband's collapsing in her arms. Before his collapse he had told Darleen never to place him in a hospital. One morning her husband had an attack at the kitchen table, and she called for an ambulance. Her husband was transported to a hospital where he died a few days later. Darleen relives the incident:

> And he just passed out in my arms. It just scared me so. Maybe I'm wrong; my son says I'm wrong. I wish I had just left him there and let him die with me. Because I didn't know what to do. But I feel like—I don't think about it so much anymore because, what good does it do? I wish I had just let him stay near me because the doctor said, "Just one more day would have been too late to take him to the hospital because he was almost gone."

Darleen's recollection indicates a resistance to biographical reconstruction. If she was fully engaged in biographical reconstruction, she might reconstruct her memory in such a way that she could see the limits of the situation or, at least, to identify the way her judgment of the incident or herself has changed. Absent from her narrative are such biographical reconstruction phrases as, "I can see now that I was wrong," or "I didn't realize it at the time but now I know I did everything I could."

Finally, Sister Agnes, who set the tone for the group, spoke of her own life as a "progression":

> For me, for myself, when I reflect back on my life, I see—the good things come to my mind when I look back on it. And like it's a progression. What I have now is in my life because of what was in my life in the past. I have thought about this many times. My memories, some of them are awful! But they don't really glare up and put the others out of sight. I just think, well, that's the way of life.

Sister Agnes concluded:

> And as I said, I am so grateful for what I have in my life now, that when I look back, I wouldn't have changed anything, no matter what it was, for what I have now.

Paula, the woman who became Catholic in the 1970s, did indicate biographical reconstruction. She spoke of the trauma of her early childhood. Her family was anti-Christian. Her brothers and sisters were arsonists who would burn churches. Her father was a "psychopath."

She said, "But I can see that what I was there as a child, I am not even the same person. We change in every possible way, I think."

Paula was one of two members of the prayer group who mentioned dramatic religious experiences. Paula mentioned both seeing dead relatives and having out-of-body experiences of ecstasy throughout her life. She said of her mother, "My mother died when I was a baby of eighteen months, and I've missed her all my life, and I am sure I have seen her, and I think she has been with me most of the years." Yet she claimed not to have had a religious conversion. She recalled the Protestant practices of public expressions of religious conversion in her childhood and concluded, "I think that...religion, basically, deeply is within oneself. You don't parade it in front of people."

Even though Paula did not have a religious conversion, she clearly links her becoming Catholic with biographical reconstruction. Her story indicates that biographical reconstruction, as well as being a motivating force for religious change, can also be a result of religious change. I asked her if she looked back on her life and memories any differently since becoming Catholic. She responded enthusiastically, "Oh yes. Oh, definitely. Catholicism has a long view of things." She then described how Catholicism had resulted in a changed perception of her psychopathic father:

> Oh, yes, here you look to the source, you look at what it leans against, and I can understand people; my father, for instance, when I—The evidence became absolutely clear to me, and sometimes my own half brother and sister had to point it out to me. I had—My love for him was so deep that I would think, Well, Papa was...a psychopath. But after I became—started studying Catholicism, the—you bring up the question, Why, why was he a psychopath? His birth, over which he had no control—He was— His mother was—This was way back in the 1800s. You see, about 1870, when he was born. And his mother died before he was born, and they had—they don't think that...he would live. And it took a day or two to get this child to take any food, and so it was something that was in his brain and in his system over which he had no control. But he was a very vicious and very mean man. But there is a reason for it and, here again, in Catholicism you trust God. As I said, God doesn't make mistakes. And you say, "But why did this happen?" These things do happen because we have

not progressed far enough, like the AIDS. We know that we are eventually going to find a way to prevent and cure AIDS; now we don't have it. But the Catholic trusts in God that this is going to be worked out. There it has made a big difference. Whereas as a Methodist, I used to blame everybody, you know, and that isn't the correct way to look at it.

Paula has reconstructed her memories of her father. She sees Catholicism as the facilitator of reconstruction by giving her a broader view and trust in God's will.

The fact that Paula indicated a biographical reconstruction, while other members of the prayer group did not, and the fact that the RCIA participants, in general, showed greater evidence of biographical reconstruction when compared to the prayer group members, seem to support the notion in conversion literature that converts engage in biographical reconstruction in ways that are far more evident when compared to lifelong Christians. However, conversion literature focuses on the importance of religious conversion, and Paula did not claim to have had a religious conversion. Her life has changed since becoming a Roman Catholic and adopting the worldview of Catholicism. This has been accomplished in her life without an explicit religious conversion. The comparison with the prayer group suggests that focusing on the link between religious conversion and biographical reconstruction may be too narrow a view. Membership and adoption of new religious meaning structures, without identifiable religious conversion, are linked here with biographical reconstruction. In other words, the distinction in conversion literature between biographical reconstruction in converts and the relative lack of biographical reconstruction in lifelong Catholics is upheld in our comparison. But religious conversion as such does not account for the difference.

An avenue for future research, in trying to discover "what the difference is," is to compare the functional and structural differences between agents of secondary socialization and agents of re-socialization. In Berger and Luckmann's terms, the RCIA is an agent of re-socialization while the prayer group is an agent of secondary socialization. Secondary socialization presumes "an already formed self and an already internalized world" (Berger and Luckmann, 1967:140). The prayer group members have already been socialized into Roman Catholicism. Their experience as a prayer group is one of secondary socialization whereby previous knowledge is reinforced. In the RCIA, previously socialized individuals are re-socialized into a new system of meaning.

The initial comparisons made here between the prayer group members and RCIA participants suggest that future research could examine the structural contributions to re-socialization and secondary socialization. In other words, the experiences of the participants in each group may well be mirroring the diverse approaches of the prayer group and RCIA structures. The presence of biographical reconstruction in Paula's narratives may be indicative of the way she learned to deal with the past in her re-socialization as a Catholic. Such learning may be more powerful than the structures of secondary socialization she finds in the prayer group.

CONCLUSION

The stories of religious change and commitment in this chapter have yielded mixed results in considering the biographical reconstruction thesis. Biographical reconstruction has been shown to be clearly active in many individuals who also claim religious conversion. Yet some individuals who did indicate a religious conversion did not also indicate an intense biographical reconstruction that past literature would predict. The experience of the older new Catholics in this study suggests the need for precision in discussing religious conversion, membership switching, and biographical reconstruction.

An initial comparison with a prayer group of older Catholics has also challenged the strong link of biographical reconstruction and religious conversion in literature. In general, for the older new Catholics in this study, religious conversion is not a decisive issue. Membership in a religion (expressed as "becoming Catholic," "joining the Catholic Church," or "joining the RCIA") is a far more important concept. The resistance of the people I interviewed to the notion of religious conversion is even more remarkable given the RCIA's insistence that religious conversion be part of the RCIA process.

As the next two chapters will discuss, the stories of older new Catholics call us to move beyond a monocausal theory of religious conversion toward theoretical insights that more accurately reflect the diversity of experience in religious conversion and denominational

Stories of Biographical Reconstruction 65

membership switching. Ironically, where society stereotypes old age as a time of "sameness" when people think, act, and even look alike, the stories we have heard here, and will hear in the next chapters, are marked by their diversity and life.

Notes

1. The concern for maintaining the RCIA only for those who belong is reminiscent of Berger and Luckmann's discussion of insiders and outsiders. Outsiders are threats to the universe of meaning the RCIA presents (1967: 87). Many older new Catholics referred to "insider" and "outsider" saying that even though they had been attending mass for up to forty years, they still felt like outsiders because they were not members of the church.

2. Despite the unified vision of conversion and membership presented in the RCIA, Catholic literature does recognize the possibility that the vision presented will not be adopted by all participants:

> What cannot be assumed is that every catechumen is ready to be elected to participation in the Easter sacraments. In spite of every effort to make the process of initiation a true conversion of life, a real journey in faith, a deep process that involves more than just intellectual understanding, it is quite possible that a number of catechumens can come to the time of election as if it were the time of exams. (Kemp, 1979:126)

3. Consistencies remain despite Ben's claim of radical change from his pre-Catholic life. Ben linked drinking alcohol closely with his social life prior to becoming a Catholic. A large prominent bar in his home stands as a testimony to the place of alcohol in his life. Pointing to the bar he told me:

> I stood there and learned the Lord's Prayer....I never knew the Lord's Prayer. And I remember I got it and I said I can say this prayer. And I never knew that was the Lord's Prayer they say in church. I really didn't. But I learned it standing right there at that bar. I memorized it. "Hey, I can say that." I said it to her [wife]; I memorized it, you know.

4. Given the institutional favor shown to biographical reconstruction in the RCIA (as detailed above), people who strongly demonstrated biographical reconstruction could be said to be engaged in "a reciprocal typification of

habitualized actions..." (Berger and Luckmann, 1967:54). That is, there is a reciprocity of institutional typifications (RCIA support structures for biographical reconstruction), typical actors (individuals seeking to reconstruct their biographies) and typical actions (personal and group efforts at biographical reconstruction). In short, the social reconstruction of biography is institutionalized in the RCIA process.

5. Of the sixteen people who did not strongly indicate a biographical reconstruction, only nine indicated they had had a religious conversion. Three indicated they did not have a religious conversion. The remaining four neither affirmed nor denied a religious conversion. Thus, nine individuals who indicated they had had a religious conversion did not strongly indicate biographical reconstruction. The intensified and amplified reconstruction that Snow and his associates detailed is not present in these nine stories. The link of religious conversion and biographical reconstruction is broken in this group.

6. The symbolic universe of the RCIA has served to legitimate both Cathy's individual biography (with the conflicts presented by Mark's death) and the institutional order of the Catholic Church (which placed Mark's death in a plausibly meaningful context). In Berger and Luckmann's words, "The symbolic environment provides order for the subjective apprehension of biographical experience. Experiences belonging to different spheres of reality are integrated by incorporation in the same, overarching universe of meaning" (1967:97).

7. The specific contributions of the RCIA in providing a meaningful context for the reconstruction of biography are indicated as well in Larry's words:

> There's a very powerful feeling and I later, many years later, after I had gone through the RCIA, and been taught about the Holy Spirit, I thought it must be the Holy Spirit. Maybe it was that, I don't know, I'll never know, but it felt like that must have been what it was. It gave me that sense of well-being that I was in tune with Christ and with the Church even though there were difficulties.

8. Berger and Luckmann state that once individuals become members of a religious community through conversion, the new members must be careful with whom they talk: "Outsiders who used to be biographically significant are still dangerous" (1967:159). The old reality they invoke may tempt the new members. Despite these warnings, and the hints of outsider temptation implied in Cathy's remarks, the Catholic Church does not limit interaction with

outsiders. In my field observations the only limits noticeable were the limits in interaction caused by the devotion of time and energy by the participants of the RCIA. That is, they may not have made an explicit decision not to associate with others, but with the new RCIA acquaintances, they may not have had the time or energy for former relationships.

3
Beyond Biographical Reconstruction

Biographical reconstruction, religious conversion, and membership switching do not occur in social vacuums. Rather, a mutual relationship exists whereby the individual at once utilizes social structures in an effort to find meaning in life and is influenced by those social structures. Chapters 3 and 4 will examine a number of motivating factors that help answer the question, why do older people join the Catholic Church? In addressing this question we will pay particular attention to the mutual relationship (or dialectic) between social reality and the individual (Berger and Luckmann, 1967:187).

As was the case in our discussion of biographical reconstruction, the dynamics involved in joining a religion will largely be told by the participants in the study. Their words and experiences will be cited to clarify and exemplify motivating factors and the social dialectic. We will present the story of becoming Roman Catholic in the words and impressions of the people I interviewed. The stories of religious change and commitment are told more in terms of membership in the Catholic Church than in terms of religious conversion.

From these stories six motivating factors for becoming Catholic emerged in addition to biographical reconstruction. This chapter examines the four factors that are related to the life cycle: facing developmental issues of aging, embracing a seeker mentality, dealing with crises or transitions in life, and integrating early childhood memories. Chapter 4 will examine the influence of significant others particularly in families and in social groups. In other words, Chapter 3 will focus more on the individual aspects of the dialectic and Chapter Four will focus more on the social aspects of the dialectic.

Even though the six factors are largely presented separately, as Dot's story in the opening pages of this book indicated, often no single factor could be identified as more powerful an explanation than any other for individuals or for the participants in this study as a whole. These six factors often combined into a complex decision to become Roman Catholic. Additionally, the separation of individual and social factors is for the purpose of analysis. As the concept of a dialectic implies, in everyday life the individual and social are intertwined.

AGE

Why *Other* Older People Become Catholic: Facing Issues of Life and Death

The most unique feature of the new Catholics I interviewed is that society has dubbed them to be "old." Facing issues of aging is a reality for everyone. The dynamics of age, and the uniqueness of their stories as *older* new Catholics, were evident in the stories they told.

Despite the reality of old age, few people admitted their joining the Catholic Church was related to their age. Yet almost every person I spoke with offered insight into why *other* people might become Catholic in later life. One man answered the question "Is there a reason why you did it [joined the church] now in your life?" very defensively: "No. One thing I didn't want, I didn't want anyone to think that I was doin' this because I was getting old and might die."

Lula, the woman in the midst of a biographical reconstruction, linked the process of joining the church with old age. Speaking about why other older individuals might join the church Lula stated, "Well, I think probably as you get older, you start looking at your life. And also you know you are looking at that line also." She concluded, "But I am sure…that death is coming around the corner and that maybe perhaps running after the almighty dollar is not the way of life. That they would like to change their life." Lula's speculation links the influence of age with the life review and biographical reconstruction.

Similar to Lula, many people related facing death and eternal life with the decision to become Catholic in later life. Larry, the sixty-five-year-old retired computer systems manager, suggested:

As you get older, you think maybe I better get things squared away [laughing] before it is too late. That's probably a factor too. You know, very realistically you have enough debate in you about this issue of I've got to fish or cut bait here, you know. I think as you get older that is something you better face up to and decide, you know. Are you going to buy this and be part of it, or aren't you? You know. Let's make a decision here.

Edna commented:

> Because they realize they are coming to—their days are numbered, their years are numbered, and something has told them that they must be accountable to God for the life they led, what they did and what they didn't do....

Unresolved Conflicts in Later Life

Ben, who described himself in the last chapter as being a "rowdy dude" in his pre-baptism life and said he was afraid of dying before his baptism but not anymore, also spoke about the resolution of unresolved conflicts in his life. Recall that unresolved conflicts are another key aspect of the life review. He said that in baptism he felt the burden of his sins being lifted from his shoulders. Ben's baptism was a public and social manifestation of the resolution of unresolved conflicts. He described the ceremony in this way:

> Well, like I say, five hundred pounds come off my shoulders. I would say that, let me put it that way, and I could stand and look out at all the people out there and not drop my head; I was lookin' right in the faces and smilin', you know what I'm saying?

Ben was the second person who spoke of looking in a mirror. Ben told me, now that he was Catholic, "I can look myself in a mirror, I look myself in the face; it feels good like a—I feel that a heavy burden has been lifted off my shoulders and things are just great." Additionally, Ben told of an exercise in the RCIA group in which he was looking at a book of faces of Jesus. The last page of the book was a mirror with the inscription, "So many different faces of Jesus, this is the face you'll always see." Ben said this experience "made a real big difference to me." He said, "It really hit me hard; I had tears going down my cheeks, believe me. I felt so different to look in the mirror and to see that."

Beyond Biographical Reconstruction

Ben noticed age differences in the way people in his group dealt with the mirror exercise: "I was watching the young ones. When the mirror came to them, they just [Ben clapped his hand, indicating a swift closing of the book] passed it on."[1]

Age-Related Expectations and Issues

Age was identified as relating to some other effects. Lenny indicated that being older might place added pressure on individuals to meet expectations and may be an added social motivation to complete the RCIA process:

> Y'know, when you wait forty-odd years and you go into a program, it's pretty hard to say, "No, I really don't think it's for me," because it's—well, I think I would have been—I would have been ashamed of myself, really.

Finally, Pierre directly relates his decision to become Catholic with his age (sixty-five):

> *Did becoming Catholic when you did have anything to do with your age?*
>
> Well, I would say so. I was probably more settled down and I said at that point that "I gotta do somethin' before I get too old," y'know. "I gotta have a goal and a path, a straight path to go on, so I better quit foolin' around and—and straighten out everything in my life, in a religious way." I was always kinda religious, but, I kinda was a staggered walkway—I wasn't straight.

Thus the urge to "straighten out everything in my life," to make sense of one's biography and one's world, became more immediate and evident as the people in this study got older. They were active in trying to face the challenge to meaning that growing old often poses. They found in the Catholic Church a plausible way of dealing with the challenges of the aging process.

Age as an Obstacle

For some, being older presented some obstacles. Bud spoke of being offended by a comment of the RCIA director about his age:

> Yeah, this Tim [RCIA Director] said "At your age, what did you join the church for?" I said, "Well, I don't know; I wanted to be a Catholic, that's all." I didn't have any reason. But he asked me that and it kind of ticked me off.

Oh, because he said, "At your age?"

> Yeah, he said, "At your age, why would you?" It was the way he said it: "Why would you want to become a Catholic?" I said, "Well, it's as good a time as any, as far as I know. I could have become a Catholic twenty years ago or forty years ago; it wouldn't have made any difference."

Gloria, still an active lawyer at age seventy-six, described a general feeling of being out of place because she was older:

> You know, it is interesting when you are older. You always have the feeling that people think, Why is she doing this because she is older? Like lots of times now, not a lot of times, but occasionally I will have people say, "What? You are still practicing law?" as if I should not be doing this, that I should be home. And that's kind of the feeling that I had in the RCIA....There were a couple of older people, but we all had the feeling that, because there were many young people there, that there was not the place for us, that there should be some other place.

The uniqueness of being older in the RCIA was evident when Gloria addressed the congregation on the night she was baptized. A small but stately woman, Gloria approached the pulpit with confidence. The congregation was particularly attentive given that we had already been in the church for over three hours. Gloria's voice was surprisingly strong given her small stature:

> I am pleased to share with you, as one of the older members of the RCIA, the exhilarating and moving experience of the journey, which in my case encompassed one year. How, you may wonder, does one in later years become interested in embarking on such a journey? In my case the Lord was watching over me, and it was happenstance.
>
> Being older can confound the need for belonging. By becoming

Catholic in later life, these people were betraying the social expectations of literature and common perception regarding age-appropriate behavior. Individuals are supposed to switch religions in adolescence and young adulthood. I asked one RCIA director if she noticed a rift between older and younger participants in the RCIA. She said there was not a "rift" but there was initially a feeling that the older people do not belong. She said that an older married couple in her group was initially mostly ignored by the younger participants, but now they had become the "favored couple." At first people would not talk to them at all, but now that they had become known, everybody wanted to talk to them. Thus, from this RCIA director's perspective, the age barriers were real, but temporary.

The RCIA can be an age-neutralizing reality; that is, status is attained through membership, and membership is not determined by age. However, age does become an issue when participants are "pushed through" the RCIA at a faster pace because they are older. Thus, age can be at once a motivator for becoming Catholic, an obstacle for becoming Catholic, and a way of enhancing "the journey" toward Catholicism.

The Perceived Rootedness of the Catholic Church and the Perceived Rootlessness of Old Age

Many individuals mentioned the rootedness, history, or formality of Roman Catholicism as being attractive. Deb suggested the Catholic Church offered "strength and guidance." Furthermore, she suggested that the church offered a "structure that a lot of people like and need as they get older...."

Reverend Jones told of his dismay over the "proliferation" of Protestant denominations compared to the fact that "every Catholic church that I've ever known about in my lifetime" is still alive and going strong. "That's one of the things historically I like about the Catholic Church." Helen spoke of factions within her former Presbyterian faith and in Protestantism in general, "And I thought, all of these religions— it's strange, but they're all fighting within themselves, and I wanted something I felt that I could hold on to, and that's really the, the basis of it all." Liza compared the Episcopal and Catholic Churches and concluded, "Why not go to the source?" Liza said the major thing that attracted her to Roman Catholicism was "the feeling of continuity from the time of Christ. I'm part of the church that has existed through the ages." Additionally, Liza found the teachings of the Catholic Church attractive, "So I particularly liked that, that I knew where the church stood on something, and therefore I knew where I should be."

Particularly addressing the RCIA, James Dunning suggests that the renewal in zest for church history, along with emphases on roots and genealogies, is a sign "that a people who have felt rootless are now searching for the 'whence' of their story" (1979:150). Implied in these stories is the possibility that the social, physical, and personal diminishments of age may contribute to feeling "rootless." For these older new Catholics, the Catholic Church offers a return to roots.

The appeal of the rootedness of the church is implied in other images presented in the stories of becoming Catholic. Judy is a tall and confident seventy-one-year-old retired bank teller. The intonation of her voice, her stature, and her personal approach all indicate a calm at the center of her life. Yet her life story is marked by phenomenal tragedy. She had spent years with an abusive alcoholic man. She had a daughter with this man, who, Judy said, molested her daughter. Her daughter was kidnapped as a teenager and has been having constant struggles with drug abuse and mental health as an adult. Judy herself once attempted suicide. She remarried later in life to an active Catholic. She began attending Catholic services with her husband and enjoyed the "formality to the religion." She said, "I liked the formal religion," and concluded, "I enjoy being a Catholic because it gives me a lot of consolation and it gives me a set program like when you go to church and pray, and I do that every Sunday."

The "consolation" Judy mentioned was echoed in other interviews. I heard stories of a "lifeline" to hold onto or simply "something to hold onto." Judy related this consolation to the life-review issue of facing death. The link with age comes in the fact that dealing with issues of death becomes a more immediate task as one grows older.

What does it mean to you to be a Catholic now?

Well, I feel like I'm—You know it's like...life is a box. And you jump around, in and out, in and out of the box, in and out of trouble, in and out of peace, and I feel like I'm in a nice cozy box where my future is taken care of. I know that if there is a hereafter I am going to be there.

Judy's description of Catholicism as "a nice cozy box" captures the appeal that the social structure of Roman Catholicism offers to these older new Catholics. At the end of our interview Judy stated the crux of the issue: "It gave me a feeling of security; that's why I became Catholic."[2]

Bringing Judy's experience into dialogue with Berger and Luckmann, we can see a link between the life review, the RCIA structure, and Judy's sense of security. Berger and Luckmann state that the ordering of different phases of biography is supported by symbolic universes which are "conducive to feelings of security and belonging" (1967:99). Judy, concerned about death, and about the enormous struggles of her life, found meaning in the symbolic universe of the Catholic Church. In the Catholic Church she found a secure environment in which to engage her life review and to order her biography. All these issues are intensified as one ages and comes to recognize that the time to face these issues is slipping away.[3]

The security Judy finds in the structural aspects of the church, in this case from the sacrament of confession, has direct impact on her own life review:

> Now I understand...that I don't have to go to confession unless I feel I have done something, or even if I just want to. Something bothering me from the past I can get it off my chest, and make me feel a little less burdened by something that has happened in the past, which I might—I have wished I could have changed, but at the time I didn't know why—why things happened the way they do. Who knows? That's the way I did it. I made a mistake; I made a few, plenty of mistakes....

Dealing with mistakes and issues of one's past in the face of death is common in the stories of older new Catholics. Clara, at age seventy-one, stated, "The older you get, the closer you think of maybe of dying or something like that, and the more you realize the important things from the unimportant."

Death and Finite Time

Clara's statement is reminiscent of Berger and Luckmann's discussion of death. They suggest the knowledge of the inevitability of death makes time finite for individuals. The limited time available to accomplish one's projects is realized. The individual approaches his/her projects with a greater sense of urgency and anxiety. The authors state, "My waiting will be anxious to the degree in which the finitude of time impinges upon the project" (1967:27).

The urgency of facing life's projects is reflected in those individuals who cited a lifelong desire or knowledge that they would become Catholic. The knowledge of the inevitability of death, and the finitude of biographical time, may have prompted a final dealing with this life project.

Furthermore, Berger and Luckmann suggest, "A strategic legitimating function of symbolic universes for individual biography is the 'location' of death" (1967:101), and "The integration of death within the paramount reality of social existence is, therefore, of greatest importance for any institutional order" (1967:101). Roman Catholicism integrates the phenomenon of death within its symbolic universe. Such integration is both an attraction for new members and a source of legitimation for individual biographies.

RCIA participants are encouraged to face issues of life and death in the context of belief in God. For example, an RCIA training video links facing issues of death with the search for meaning. This same link is drawn in life-review literature. After presenting the story of a nun named Thea, who is dying of cancer, the narrator says:

> But the reality of dying makes Thea want to attach a final significant meaning to her existence. Her lifelong goal has been a simple one, to know, love and serve her God. But questions persist: Did she make a difference? Did she make a significant mark with the life she had to live? (RCIA Starter Stories Video, Volume One, 1991)

The legitimation of death which Roman Catholicism and the RCIA present is evident in the stories two men told of attending Catholic funeral services. They were impressed with the services enough to get them thinking about becoming Catholic. I asked Bud, "Had you thought about becoming Catholic before being impressed by the services that Father Fred had offered?" He replied:

> Well, my wife used to talk to me about it and I thought about it, but it didn't impress me much, and so I just kind of passed it away and

let it go at that. Until he came along. It seemed like I guess after I knew him, all the people I knew who were older were passing away and the more funerals we had just kind of kept snowballing.

The resolution of issues of death by becoming Catholic seems total in many cases. As Bud proclaimed, "If I was going to die tomorrow, it wouldn't bother me a bit." However, for some the fear of death still remains. I asked Sally, "Is there anything that frightens you about the future?" She responded:

I suppose death does, because I am so uncertain about what's going to happen after the time comes: whether we will we go right to heaven or will we wait until Christ comes or just what will happen.

The way these people dealt with issues of death exemplifies the social dynamic. The church presents a legitimating social structure for facing issues of death and the people I interviewed actively use the structure to place their thoughts about death in perspective. This is more than an elective affinity of an individual facing death and a social structure presenting a plausible explanation for death. Rather, the church and the individual are both actively seeking and revealing the meaning of death.

Old Age as a Retrospective Time

Finally, old age was portrayed as a quiet and retrospective time. The additional time and opportunity for reflection that being older presented may have facilitated consideration of membership. Gloria said she became Catholic when she did because "this was a time fairly peaceful in my life, where I could look into some kind of religious philosophy." For many of these older new Catholics, old age was the first time they had the luxury of time, introspection, and leisure to help them make sense of their lives and worlds. Having time available allowed them to consider their lives in ways they may not have previously. June linked age, joining the church, and the added time for introspection:

Do you find yourself looking back at your life any differently now than you have in the past?

Yeah. Now, again, that might be from joining the church and it also might be from getting older, about, Why the heck did we get so upset over that? Y'know, that sort of thing. Like if you could just—just take the time to think it out a bit, be a little peaceful about it.

Remarkably, Willard answered the same question with the same imagery: joining the church, being older, and finding peace.

Do you look back at your life differently now than you did at other times in your life?

Yes, I—I guess I would. I don't know if it's the age or it's becoming Catholic or what, but as I—I say, with the inner peace that I have with myself now, much more so, and I'm convinced I'm in the right direction.

Prayer Group Comparison

The relationship of age to religious dynamics was drawn by the lifelong Catholics as well. Darleen was explicit about increased reminiscence in her life. Early in our interview Darleen was speaking about the difficulties of being married and poor. She stated, "I can remember all this now that I am here alone. And as old as I am. I'm ninety-two and a half."

Later in our interview I asked,

You were saying before that being alone made you remember more?

Yes! Uh-huh. I think of all these things; I go over my life which we never had time to do before. We do things, forget about that, and go to the next thing, forget about that, and go to the next thing. But now I can look back and see all these different things.

Joan also addressed the added opportunity for reflection that comes with age:

As you get older I think you be closer to God. I feel I am much closer to the church and my...God than I was when I was younger.

> I had too many responsibilities when I was younger. As you get older you have less responsibilities when you're closer...to read more...and when you get closer to God. That's the only way I can explain it.

Karen said that the loneliness that often accompanies old age made the need for the prayer group greater in her life. Dealing with her son's cancer "can really weigh you down." She said that being alone in a room with four walls made the need to express herself even more important.

Issues of death and meaning were prominent in the prayer group. The members of the prayer group, being socialized into the Catholic teaching on death for over seven decades, spoke positively about the prospects of death. I interviewed one member on the day her sister died. She described the death as a "lovely thing." In our interview she spoke of her father's death from cancer. She said, "Thank God, I got home to see my father before he died. It was pathetic. If it was a dog you would shoot it, honestly....But that is another time I thank God for the gift of death."

Joan related some of the very practical concerns of living to her vision of dying:

> I visualize heaven sometimes...and everything is very bright... and white. I don't know why I think about white; everything is white and pure. And, I hope I get there. I don't want to go any place else but there. It must be a beautiful place. There is music; there are harps playing. There's no sorrow. It's all laughter. We don't have to lock ourselves in our homes and be afraid of somebody coming in and breaking into your home. There is so much crime out here...on this earth that you hear about it. No more earthquakes.

Darleen had a near-death experience in which she claimed to have seen a beautiful vision of heaven. She often says the prayer, "Help me God, to discover the nothingness of this world, the greatness of heaven, the shortness of time, and the length of eternity." After reciting the prayer she told me, "So when you are looking forward to something like that, how can you not think about it from time to time? When you're dead, you're dead."

In the course of six months, six close relatives of Joan, including her son and her grandson, died. Dealing with these deaths was the most prominent issue in the history of the prayer group. The group took ownership of Joan's struggles with anger at God and surrender to God. They went through these emotions with her. Joan's resolution that "God needed my son more than I did" was largely reached through talking out the deaths in the prayer group. Through her religious faith, and through the social support of the prayer group, Joan has gained a sense of meaning while confronting death.

Thus both prayer group members and RCIA participants cited increased retrospection in age as relevant to their religious pursuits. The increased time, and effort, in inward activities that came with age was a motivator for these older adults to face issues that were resolved through membership in the Catholic Church and/or increased religiosity.

Berger and Berger state, "For the individual, old age is, above all, a problem of meaning in life" (1972:327). A comparison of the RCIA participants with the prayer group members indicates that facing issues of life and death are very common in later life and may prompt religiosity.

The prayer group is portrayed as one of the very few places that older people can talk about issues of aging and find someone who listens. The prayer group also represents a place in the church for older people. The church is portrayed as neglecting the concerns of the elderly. Karen said about the church, "Older people are really excluded from everything." In the prayer group older women found a place they could talk, and talk religiously.

Aging Summary

Developmental issues of aging are a motivator for some individuals to seek membership in the Catholic Church. Once they join the RCIA, they often find roles and expectations that are strongly age-linked (Clausen, 1972:506). One's age may not only contribute to one's joining the RCIA, it may also contribute to one's remaining in the process. The linking of age-related issues and religious experience was evident as well in the lifelong Catholic members of the prayer group.

SEEKERS

In one of the few major studies of conversion to Roman Catholicism, Dean Hoge and his research team (1981) reported that one type of convert is the "seeker convert." Seeker converts are individuals who have a need that impels them to an interest in religious groups and religious study. Intermarriage, another of Hoge's types, was far more evident as a motivator for joining the church in our interviews. However, there were individuals who indicated a definitive seeker mentality.

The Older Seeker and a "Seeker Mentality"

The seeker mentality differs in these older people when compared to the seeker careers that are often cited among adolescent and young adult converts (Kilbourne and Richardson, 1989:12). Among younger converts a seeker is usually an individual who joins many different religious movements until that person finds the one movement that suits her/him. Among the later-life Catholics, seeking membership in various churches was not frequent. Rather, the elders showed a "seeker mentality" that seemed more related to a search for meaning in life (Erikson, 1982).

The seeker mentality was evident in a variety of forms. A woman who was attracted to monastic retreats said, "I kept searching and, oh, I'm a sleuth...." Her searching for spiritual renewal eventually led to a search for church membership:

> And finally I said, "Why am I going to all these retreats but not going to the church." That's what made me seek out the church; then finally, to know it better.

One man described an intellectual curiosity as he spoke of a Bible commentary he had read:

> I'm just curious; I'm intellectually curious as to why, y'know, the explanation of a lot of these things. But I got the complete set of Barclay. I've read it twice and still I have a lot of questions. I guess I'll have questions all my life.

Dave described the RCIA from a definite seeker mentality. I asked him,

"How would you describe the RCIA to someone who didn't know what it was?" He responded:

> To me, and I've done this, I tried to explain that all of us have questions about what the hereafter is. What happens to us? Is there a God? Who is God? What is God? And, y'know, you could approach this from a philosophical viewpoint or you just put all that garbage away and say, "I'm looking for something. I know there's somebody out there greater than I. Who is this?" Here's a place for you to come in, and with people just like you get the answers to that, to open up a faith journey for you to walk where you will meet God. You won't see him but you will meet him and you will know you met him—and I know I've met him.

The social character of the individual's quest to find meaning in life and afterlife is implied in Dave's description of finding a place where "people just like you get the answers." The reconstruction of his biography and world is ultimately social in nature. The familial, social, and age-related influences in becoming Catholic often coincide with a seeker mentality.

The Questioning Seeker

The social nature of the seeking is addressed by James Dunning. He states: "The overwhelming challenge and critical task in the Inquiry stage…" is to prompt questions of meaning (1981b:187).

Pierre, a Canadian-born man, spoke of the urge he felt to study Catholicism. He sat down with a priest and asked him questions about Catholicism. "I have to find out for myself, investigate it myself; this is what I've done." Pierre is an active seeker. Like many people in this study, Pierre praised the openness of the RCIA process in terms of asking questions and getting answers. The questioning that Dunning advocates is being accomplished consistently in RCIA programs.

Reverend Jones linked the openness of asking and answering questions to his age. Although he met individually with a priest for instruction, his comments regarding questions and answers are indicative of the experience of the RCIA participants. He compared an effort earlier in his life to become Catholic when he went to a nun for instruction:

> Rather than go and sit before the Mother Superior, she said, "Who made God?" I said, "He is, always was, and always will be." And we never got into any discussion of any kind; we just went through that. Whereas Monsignor and I would sit like you and I are sittin', and I'd ask him a question about Purgatory: "What about it?" And he would spend his time and then he would allow me to ask him, and that give-and-take, at my age or my stage of development, is what I need.

Implied in Reverend Jones's statement is the notion that older people, because of their age and stage of development, have specific ways in which to make sense of their world. The questions that lie at the heart of older people's attempts to make sense of their personal and social worlds need to be asked and answered in a "give-and-take" fashion. The RCIA process was conducted in such a way as to be open to the questions of meaning the participants were asking and to provide plausible answers to help the participants make sense of their social world. In the RCIA group, they could make sense of life with other people who accepted the questions and affirmed the answers.

The Religious Seeker

Reverend Jones is the clearest example in this study of a religious seeker, and the one individual who is a career seeker. His effort to reconstruct his personal and social world was explicitly religious. He was ordained a Methodist minister, converted to Episcopalian, became an Episcopal minister, and is now Catholic. He hopes to be a Catholic deacon. He described his changes of religious affiliation as "my search in the area of faith." After much thought and study he decided to become Catholic.

> But being in the eucharistic worship and the mass, I'd really be blessed by that, and that's what has attracted me more to Catholicism than anything else. I didn't have an understanding what eucharist was about in the Methodist Church. I began to approach it in the Episcopal Church; and as a minister in the Meth—Episcopal Church, it seemed like the real presence was what I believed and we weren't quite there yet; it seemed like we were playing at it and the Catholics had been doin' it all along in

the manner which seemed to be most beneficial to my own spiritual blessing, so that's about the way I approached it.[4]

As the paragraph above demonstrates, Reverend Jones was not only an active seeker, he was also the individual who most identified with Catholic doctrine. As a Methodist minister, "there were proposals being made and voted on and passed that just about turned my stomach." Reverend Jones liked the changes he observed in Vatican II and came to the conclusion, "I'm a believer, and why not make the step?" He concluded, "It seemed like God had kinda led me step by step, a natural progression to Catholicism."

The parity of belief among members was also cited by Liza. She compared her Baptist experience with that of being a Catholic: "To me, it is very important to feel that other people have the same belief as I do, whereas [as a Baptist] I would believe it but I knew those around me didn't. You see, so to be part of a community that believes the same is important to me." Both Reverend Jones and Liza came to realize that the way they defined reality did not match the way their religious organizations defined reality. Thus, instead of redefining their religious convictions, they changed groups. They discovered a reference group that matched their experience. Both engaged in an active, autonomous search for a new structure. Their personal changes in meaning resulted in a decision to change social worlds.[5]

The Social Seeker

The seekers were not necessarily seeking religious, philosophical, or intellectual answers. Some were trying to fulfill a goal of becoming a Catholic. Others were seeking social affirmation. Deb exemplified this search:

> I mean, when I first felt this real need, I was needing to feel more—It's hard to describe; I'm not really good at this. Just to feel love and to—I'm very capable of giving love, but I want— and I was reaching for something that has just fulfilled some things I was really needing.

As Chapter 4 details, the active search for social belonging and social affirmation was a prominent theme among these RCIA participants.

The Passive Seeker

Research in the sociology of conversion associates being a seeker with being an active convert. In this study one woman emerged as a "passive seeker." Clara was raised in the Christian Science Church and married a Catholic. From the day she married she abandoned Christian Science and went to church with her husband. They raised their children Catholic and then, after forty years of attending the Catholic Church, Clara joined. She told me how she came to that decision:

> I thought, I really had to boil it down, and I did not join the church until my girls were both married, and it came to me. And all that time, say, when the girls were going through St. James' Grammar School and West Covina High School, I would, y'know, discuss it with myself, tryin' to figure out. But I felt that if I joined the church for my husband, or joined the church so that Daddy and I could both be buried in the same place, or if I joined it for my child, that's not a very good reason. I just felt like that....So I just said my prayers and I just said, "Well, dear Lord, someday will you kindly let me know if I'm supposed to or not," because I did learn one thing in my life and that's patience....

Clara attributed her decision to finally become Catholic to a growing religious awareness. A concept she had heard often at mass is named, endorsed, and accepted as her own.[6] She recalled the time she asked her children:

> "Do you realize what really happened on Good Friday?" It really got to me, y'know. So I knew I was thinking deeply. So it did come to me, and I think the reason I joined is, I listened so many times to the sermon and mass, where it says, "Eat this bread and drink this wine, you do it for me and what I have done for you." And I thought, Oh, my, that's it right there; that's my answer! He really has, because God has been good to me. I had to wait a long time for a few things, but he's been good to me, and he's answered. Any important prayers have always been answered, and I thought, Well, I think, I gotta show you that I can do something for you, and I mean it. That's—That's really what got me going, right there.[7]

The sociological vision that Berger and Luckmann present in *The Social Construction of Reality* incorporates the fact that individuals are "seekers." We all seek meaning in our personal and social lives. We all seek to make sense of our experience. The individuals in this study indicated such a seeker mentality in their attraction to Roman Catholicism and in their attempt to order their social and personal lives. At the RCIA team day, team members were told that RCIA participants are "believers trying to make meaning of life in light of the Gospels." As Clara's interview indicates, often the search for meaning is combined with other motivating factors.

RCIA Seekers, Prayer Group "Finders"

The distinctive nature of the seeker mentality among the new Catholics is evident when comparisons are made with the prayer group of veteran Catholics. The prayer group has far more members who have *found* meaning and context for their lives than individuals seeking meaning. Roman Catholic religiosity provides the meaning structure for these members.

One member talked about the function that "only Roman Catholicism" could fulfill in her life. For example, she said, her life had changed since she heard an Easter Sunday homily on having a "heart of stone." She said that because of Roman Catholicism she had "avoided despair." These women were not seeking religious meaning; they had found answers that, for them, "only Roman Catholicism" could provide.

In the prayer group, Catholic frames of reference were used to place life events into perspective. Ellen said, "When one door closes, another door opens." Karen said, "Everything is mixed with mercy." Joan's words capture the importance of a religious framework found in her life:

> If you don't believe in God what do you have to live for? I don't know. I know prayer helped me through. I prayed a lot. And I still pray the rosary; the rosary means a lot to me. I just don't know how these people—Who do they turn to when they don't believe in anything? Life is meaningless if you don't believe in anything. This is it! And I know that there is a better place than this. That's why—Well, you think you are going through all these bad times and there has to be a better place that's waiting for you, if you behave yourself. That's my feeling.

After detailing the trials of her life, Karen said that she was "very much at peace with myself." She added, "No, I feel I am very well adjusted to my age and to what God has in store for me." I asked, "Now, someone else who lived your life, and who had some of the difficulties you had, might not be at peace, and might not be well-adjusted. What's the difference?" She responded in a fashion that is indicative of the importance of religious faith in her life: "Well, they have not wholly accepted God's will. When I feel wrong, or if I feel briefly unhappy, I always say a prayer and say, 'Well, it's God's will.'"

Paula, the only member of the group who is not a lifelong Catholic, indicated that she used to be a seeker. Her becoming Catholic was marked by constant reading about the church. She said, "In the reading I saw that Catholics had the answers that I had been longing for but could not find in other religions." Now Paula's life is framed by her desire to "cling to Christ" and "cling to the church."

One tangible indication of the distinction between seeking and finding, as well as evidence of Catholic socialization, was the prominence of religious signs and symbols in the lives of the prayer group members when compared to the new Catholics. Each prayer group member wore some religious sign, usually a cross, on her clothes. Ellen talked about a crucifix being the first piece of "furniture" she and her husband bought. In the homes of new Catholics religious symbols were hard to find, and more generic. A "Bless This House" sign would be more indicative of an older new Catholic's home. A statue of Mary would be found in a prayer group member's home.

Seekers Summary

A definitive seeker mentality was evident in some of the stories older new Catholics told of becoming Catholic. They described their journey to Roman Catholicism as being marked by seeking answers to questions, religious meaning, and social support. Although at the prayer meetings all three of these aspects were evident, the participants largely evidenced a "finder" mentality.

CRISIS OR TRANSITION PERIODS IN LIFE

David O'Rourke boldly claims, "Conversion is not essentially a religious phenomenon; it is a human mechanism for conflict resolution that is often set in a religious context" (1987:13). Although this claim seems reductionist and overstated, there are individuals in this study who dealt not only with the resolution of unresolved conflicts in their life stories, but also with recent crises or major transitions in their lives.[8]

When Everyday Life is Interrupted

A period of transition has been defined as "a span of time in which an individual's or family's normal everyday behavior patterns are disrupted by some irregular event that requires an unfamiliar response" (Charles Arn cited in Hoge, 1981:211). For some of the older new Catholics the decision to join the Catholic Church came at a transition time in their lives: retirement, unusual pressures at home and work, adjusting to widowhood. In these times the personal and social meaning that have sustained individuals may be challenged. The old answers no longer relate to the new questions that are being posed through the crisis or transition. As Berger and Luckmann suggest:

> The validity of my knowledge of everyday life is taken for granted by myself and by others until further notice, that is, until a problem arises that cannot be solved in terms of it. As long as my knowledge works satisfactorily, I am generally ready to suspend doubt about it. (1967:44)

Although James Birren is speaking about his own work in guiding autobiographies, his comments regarding transitions in later life are relevant to our study, to the autobiographical component of the RCIA, and to the relation those transitions may have to one's becoming Catholic:

> For many older adults, life changes such as widowhood and retirement can damage feelings of identity and self-worth. Guided autobiography is ideally suited to foster in the older adult a belief that his or her life is meaningful and something of which to be proud (Birren and Deutchmann, 1991:ix).

A bishop's address to RCIA team members hints at a relationship between meaning structures and life experience. Berger and Luckmann suggest that new life experiences may demand new meaning structures.

The bishop says, "The normal challenges of daily life are constantly impacting on these new inquirers." Implied in his words is the notion that the new meaning structure of the RCIA may impact their life experience.

Death of a Loved One

Reverend Jones was the only person who named the present day as the "worst time" of his life. His reflections on this time capture both Berger and Luckmann's notion of the challenge to "everyday life" and Birren and Deutchmann's claim of the challenge to identity and meaning presented by major transitions in later life:

> [Sigh] This has been one of the worst times, since November last, when my wife died....I don't like living—This would not be the life for me, once you've been married for so many years, and I don't like being a—living alone, but my daughter has moved back and living with me; that's not gonna be forever, but she's a teacher and not married, so—Oh yeah, it's tough being a widower, y'know, losing your wife. She had cancer so it was over a period of two or three years—that whole period's a bad scene, tough, my faith.

Reverend Jones admitted that he came to the Catholic Church at "a tough period." He said that he did not know how to deal with the death of his wife and "I needed somebody to minister to me at that time...."

Suicidal Thoughts

Three of the older new Catholics had contemplated suicide at one time in their lives. Liza described her "looking for God" immediately following a suicide attempt. She and her husband were raising five teenagers. They had "financial reverses" which resulted in their income dropping below the poverty level. Liza said that she began relying on alcohol and "becoming a very ugly person." Liza set up her car with an exhaust hose to the window; she turned on the engine and the radio. "And this Christian radio program came on, and something made me listen to that for a half an hour. And by the end of that I said, 'I can't go ahead with this; I just can't.' So I went back home again. And then I began looking for God again." Although she loved the Catholic Church, her husband objected to Catholicism; thus they joined the

Lutheran Church. She described this experience of twenty-five years ago as a "conversion experience." Since then her life has changed; the conversion experience has remained with her.

Liza told how the result of her conversion experience mitigated the trauma in her life:

> I think the thought that I was forty and I really hadn't felt successful in life was traumatic for me. So I kind of remember, life is supposed to begin at forty; I don't see it beginning. But after I really found God again, it was life began at forty again.

Liza is a clear example of an individual who used religious concepts and faith to combat crisis in her life.

Dramatic Personal Confrontations

Edna became a Catholic soon after she discovered her husband was homosexual: "My husband and I, and the trauma that we went through, is part of the reason I guess why I finally ended up in the Catholic Church." Edna was told her husband was homosexual by one of his coworkers, and she reacted with anger and bitterness: "I began to feel that I had been violated, used as a respectable front for someone who really wanted to be somebody else." She began taking daily walks that brought her by a Catholic church and noticed that it was "always open." Her coming upon the church was not mere coincidence; she said she was "looking for warmth or something. I was looking for something." Later in our interview she said, "I wanted to meet people; I felt very isolated."

The episode with her husband led Edna to the church. Once she got there she found many things she liked: the friendliness of the people, the childhood memory of something unobtainable in Catholicism, the emphasis on the mass and Mary, and her perception of the church as a "growing organism." Her meaning structure as a wife was shattered when she discovered her husband was homosexual. Her new meaning structure was found in the Catholic Church.

The discovery of her husband's homosexuality was certainly a motivation for Edna to become Catholic. Her reflections on what she had learned in the process is an example of the difficulty of separating in reality the distinctions of theory. That is, her words indicate crisis and trauma in her life, biographical reconstruction, and a seeker mentality:

> That was my biggest problem with my husband, and I have confessed this, and I will again to you, to Father Phil, and I feel that I was extra-hard on Ralph on account of false pride without recognizing—feeling somehow I should have—this should not have happened to me. But it did; it happened. But it also happened to him, and he explained to me, my husband did: it was not a happy thing to be who he is. And after I realized that I had been somewhat cool about it all, I began to see that my own pride and ego were involved in it and I decided that I had not asked the Holy Spirit enough questions and so that's it.

These reflections were prompted by the question, "What does it mean for you to be a Catholic?" Edna indicates that through Roman Catholicism she has come to reconstruct responsibility and blame in the crisis episode. Biographical reconstruction is clearly evident in her words "after I realized" and "I began to see." Her seeker mentality is indicated in the "questions" she needed to ask of the Holy Spirit.

Recovering from Illness

Ben spoke of how his bout with cancer led to his becoming Catholic. Answering the question, "Can you tell me how you happened to become Catholic?" he stated:

> I prayed when I had cancer. I talked to "The Man" and he brought me through. I figured, Hey, maybe he's tryin' to tell me some'n': "You're a heathen, Mister; you're a heathen. You'd better do some'n' about your life, straighten it out." And I think that's the thing that did it.

Prior to the onset of his cancer Ben did not practice any religion. His experience of praying and then surviving cancer meant the non-religious social world he had constructed was no longer suitable to his experience.

Past Crises and Transitions

Some individuals spoke of transitions and crises in the distant past in relation to their becoming Catholic. Helen, for example, who is blind, spoke about the perspective that age, religion, and sharing life stories could bring to crises.

How do you feel about sharing your own life story?

> I think it's good; I really do. As I said before, some of the things are so tragic, and I look at young people and the things they talk about and they're so tragic at the time; but as life goes on, they're not that tragic. And if you can, with God's help, work over these things, it makes it much easier and you grow from it. It's a growing experience. So I don't mind at all.

By saying "with God's help," Helen indicates the religious nature of the perspective she has gained.

In the section above on age, the importance of a sense of peace was discussed. Ida related that sense of peace to the ongoing transitions and crises of life:

What does it mean for you to be a Catholic today?

> Well, I have, like, peace of mind and I'm content. Like, before this I was never really content; I was, like I said, in the Protestant religion; I was never really content with it. I was always—Where now when I go to church, I'm as peaceful as can be. If anything happens to me, I seem to be able to—You know, I cope with it much better, knowing that the Lord is always with me. That's how it is.

The peaceful feeling that comes from the church, can you put into words what that comes from?

> No, I really can't. Just as soon as I go into church it's, you know, everything that has gone on, or is on the outside, disappears.

Although Ida cannot put the source of her feelings of peace into words, she does speak with confidence and conviction of God's activity in her past. At the end of our interview I asked Ida's husband how he felt about his wife joining him in the Catholic Church. He said, "Oh great!" and then told the story of how they met:

> [Ida's husband]: And I was a widower and I used to go to St. Phillip's by myself, and I used to pray that he would either take my life...[he begins crying].

[Ida]: Oh, he's going to cry [nervously laughing]. We both prayed for the same thing because being a widow or widower is a very lonely life, you know, and you are used to having a partner, you know, for so many years and then all of a sudden you're left. So you kinda feel that, you know, you either want to be led to somebody or that [to die].

Prayer Group Members: Life Crises and God's Will

For the prayer group members placing present and past crises in the perspective of God's will and their faith was a constant theme in their meetings and our interviews. At one prayer meeting Karen said, "If I didn't have God, I could not get through this." This confession of the need for God came when dealing with a relatively minor issue of coping with a sore foot. She said that even for such a "little thing" she needed God.

Trust in God's will and God's ways was the most prominent theme of the prayer group. Again and again the issues of life were brought into perspective by referring to God. When Joan's son died, she rebelled against God, but came to the conclusion, "God needed my son more than I did." When Paula lost a precious ring, she felt her prayers to Jesus directly resulted in its retrieval. Two members of the group mentioned having suicidal thoughts and surviving them because of their belief in God. Joan said, "Actually, if I did not believe in God I would have committed suicide."

The image of God as the integrating factor of life, and the source of meaning in life's crises, was so important among these elders that they could not imagine coping with the vicissitudes of life without God. Frequently each member would ask, "How can people live without God?" In each interview each prayer group member could not offer any insight on how some people coped without God in their lives.

The prayer group comparison suggests that for some people facing life transitions and crises can prompt religious perspectives. Both the prayer group members and the RCIA participants turned to religion in the face of present and past crises. The RCIA participants seemed to focus more on organized religion through membership, whereas the prayer group members relied on religious belief, especially in their images of God.

Crises and Transitions Summary

For the RCIA participants, both recent crises and dealing with the traumas of one's past are related to religious change and commitment in their later life. The church offers the individual a means to deal with life's crises, yet the presence of crises or traumas in the lives of the participants of this study were not the primary influence in becoming Catholic. Unlike Lofland and Stark's model (1965), our research does not indicate that personal strain is the reason older individuals are becoming Catholic (Long and Hadden, 1983:1).

Many older new Catholics actively used the church and religion as a way to cope with life's challenges. For lifelong Catholics, their religious beliefs served as a frame for life crises and transitions.

EARLY CHILDHOOD MEMORIES

One of the most surprising findings in this study is the frequency with which early childhood memories are mentioned as influencing the decision to become Catholic in later life. For the majority of the participants their memories of childhood during the Great Depression framed their life stories. Although the age span in the study indicates that more than one age cohort is present, still, the formative early experience of living through the Great Depression was often mentioned.[9]

Berger and Luckmann discuss the changing meaning of institutions as they are passed on from generation to generation. Their words are also applicable to the ways in which individuals in this study sought to place their childhood memories in the context of the meaning structure they embraced as new Catholics: "The original meaning of the institutions is inaccessible to them in terms of memory. It therefore becomes necessary to interpret this meaning to them in various legitimating formulas" (Berger and Luckmann, 1967:62). For many older new Catholics, becoming Catholic legitimated their early childhood memories and their early childhood memories legitimated the decision to become Catholic.

Catholic Significant Others in Early Childhood

Stories of Catholicism's formative influence in childhood seemed to add legitimacy to the decision to become Catholic in later life. Cathy is a feisty and animated sixty-three-year-old retired telephone operator.

Beyond Biographical Reconstruction 95

She described her life story with enthusiasm and in vivid imagery. She credited the role of her cousins in childhood as the *primary* force in her decision to become Catholic:

> *And in your days as a child and as a teenager, what role did religion play in your family?*
>
> None whatsoever, except my cousins were Catholic. All my cousins were Catholic. And I used to be—How can I say? I used to be free to go to church wherever I wanted, and I seemed to gravitate back toward the Catholic Church. I don't know; then I don't know. But for some reason, you know, I would go to the Nazareth Church on the corner or other churches, and I would end up going back with my cousins to Catholic church.
>
> *So when you were growing up, every now and then you would go to a Catholic church because...?*
>
> Catholic church, yeah, because for some reason there was something that kept drawing me back to the Catholic church. Now, all my cousins were cradle Catholics.

Amazingly, Cathy did not see her cousins from age nine or ten until five decades later when she was baptized. Although Cathy had not told her cousins of their influence, they did attend her baptism. Cathy categorized their presence at her baptism as "a thrill": "It was a thrill for me because I think they influenced me a lot into becoming a Catholic. I used to traipse after them to church every Sunday."

When I asked Cathy, "What attracted you to Roman Catholicism as opposed to any other religion?" she replied:

> I always felt fascinated with it as a young child, with the priests and sisters, and I just thought that they were so religious. To me they seemed like they were part of God. So that when you went to another church there were just people there.

At the end of our interview Cathy revealed the motivational link between her early childhood memories and becoming Catholic. I asked, "Did dealing with memories, or looking back at your life have anything to do with you becoming a Catholic?" She replied:

I think in a round-and-about way, yes. I think my cousins—From the time I went with my cousins, I used to envy them because I wanted to go to Catholic school. And I wanted to be a part of the church and my family wouldn't let me. And I think in the back of my mind I thought, Well, someday if I can I—you know, I am going to go on and do it. It took me sixty-one years to do it, but I finally made it.

The attitude of defiance and resolution of this unresolved conflict in Cathy's life was echoed in the final words of our interview. She spoke about the two years in the RCIA process: "That was two years, two years of love and I earned that and I am going to keep that. That's mine." The social world that Cathy wished she could have constructed as a child was at last constructed as an adult. The newly acquired meaning structure of being a Catholic is evident in Cathy's placing her memories of childhood in a legitimating context.[10]

Cathy carried the memories of her cousins with her all her life. As she described her memories I could imagine Cathy "traipsing" alongside her cousins as a child. Whether or not Cathy's memory is related to actual events sixty years ago, they are real for her today. As Cohler suggests:

Since memory is developmentally determined and is based on the totality of the life history to that particular point in development...it is no more possible to assume that the content of adult memory directly represents that of early childhood than to assume that the imagined events of childhood actually took place (1982:217).

Establishing Lifelong Patterns in Early Childhood

Liza told of her experience as a seven-year-old. She would go to church with a Catholic friend and ask her questions about the Catholic Church:

I just felt the presence of God so much in the Catholic Church that for the rest of my life I found myself gravitating back to the Catholic Church when I was under stress. Somehow that childhood experience was very important to me. And when I was looking for God, I would go looking in a Catholic church for him.

As a teenager, although active in the Baptist Church, Liza would go to the Catholic Church "when I felt I really had to find God and talk to him about some traumatic thing I was going through...." Liza concluded that ever since she was a little child she felt the Catholic Church was where she should be. For Liza the questions that stress and trauma posed in her life were answered in the Catholic Church.

Ida spoke of becoming Catholic as a fulfillment of a "lifelong dream." At age seven she decided she wanted to become Catholic and her mother intervened. After she married her first husband she tried again, but he intervened. Finally, after marrying a Catholic, she completed the RCIA process. The only explanation Ida offered for her desire to be Catholic at age seven was, "My friends were Catholics. I was never content in the Protestant Church." Ida underlined the childhood connection in her answer to the question, "Is there anything specifically about Roman Catholicism that you find attractive?" She stated, "No, just that I said from a child I was attracted to it."

Parental Influence

Some people, in telling the stories of their early childhood, underlined the importance of parental influence and how that influence translated into a movement toward Catholicism in later life. Deb, who described her father as anti-Catholic, recalled the "wonderful" and "marvelous" stories her mother used to tell about Catholicism and nuns. Such stories influenced Deb's life: "You don't even realize it at the time, but it is that much of an influence."[11]

Two women related their love for their deceased fathers with becoming Catholic. One mentioned that her parish was appealing, in part, because the priest reminded her of her father. Another individual, when asked, "What attracted you to Roman Catholicism as opposed to any other religion?" responded, "I think the colorfulness of it and the fact that I loved my father and I went many times to mass with him."

A surprising pattern among the older new Catholics was early-life traumas relating to parents: five people mentioned divorce or abandonment by their father; four, the death of their mother in childhood; four, the death of their father (one when the individual was twenty-four); one, the death of both parents; one, the absence of his father from the family due to work; and one was adopted.[12]

As in the other categories presented in this chapter, sometimes the influence of a particular motivating factor is presented as almost an afterthought. Joan, for example, when asked, "Did looking back on your life or dealing with memories have anything to do with your becoming Catholic?" said no, but added, "The only thing I can remember" was her father coming home after a work-related trip and saying, "Oh, I boarded with a good family....They were Catholic.... Oh, they were just wonderful!" Joan said, "I'll never forget that." By saying "I'll never forget that," Joan indicated the importance of that early childhood memory in her life and in her decision to become Catholic. The primary influence in her joining the Catholic Church was her companion of thirty-eight years, yet this early childhood memory relating to her father also played a part.

Childhood Memories, Life Review and Biographical Reconstruction

The influence of early childhood memories has implications for biographical reconstruction. Edna, the woman whose husband is homosexual, spoke of the many families that she knew that suffered during the Great Depression. Edna said, "The very first little playmate I recall" came from a big Catholic family. Edna used to wonder about Catholicism and "I always wished I were her and part of a big family instead of just one little girl all by herself." Edna concluded, "So I saw that their faith, as I look back on it now, was a great, great, great help to them." The connection between early childhood memories and biographical reconstruction is drawn in Edna's statement, "I always wished I were...." Now, by becoming Catholic, what she wished for has occurred. She has reconstructed her biography, so now her faith is a "great, great, great help" to her.

Later in our interview Edna gave a concise explanation as to the occurrence of early childhood memories in older people. I asked her, "Do you find yourself looking back much on your life?" She replied, "All the time." Explaining, she said, "As you get older and older and older, what happened a long time ago becomes more vivid in your mind than maybe what happened yesterday." Furthermore, she said:

> We become more engaged in thinking about our childhood maybe; we become—we go back to being children. We really always have the child inside us; that's something we have to learn to identify with. If we had hardships or hurts and things like this, those can

make very difficult times for us if we don't dig, dig, dig. It's the digging that was the hardest thing for me. I realized that when all this trauma came up with my husband that I myself just dig, to get the weeds out of my own psyche or whatever, and it's a very hard thing to face one's own self—it really, really is.

Edna concluded, "And I found comfort, I have to say, that in being in the Catholic Church faith through...the Blessed Mother. I can only say that it helped me to be able to do it; it gave me the courage to do it."

Perhaps the connection between early childhood memories and later-life religious change should not be surprising given psychological insights regarding the parallel nature of early and later life. Erik Erikson suggests youth and old age are "the times that dream of rebirth, while adulthood is too busy taking care of actual births...." (1982:80). Erikson's emphasis on rebirth suggests a uniting context in youth and old age for the possibility of religious conversion. Inasmuch as religious conversion involves rebirth, youth and old age are ideal times. Inasmuch as the life review or biographical reconstruction may prompt memories or desires for rebirth, religious conversion or denominational membership switching may be facilitated.

Early Childhood Memories and Socialization

Roof and Hoge suggest, "The strength of church-related religious socialization during a person's childhood is a determinant of one's adult attitudes and behavior" (1980:407). For the people influenced by memories of Roman Catholicism in their childhood, actually socialization may have been minimal, but recollections of that minimal socialization have become powerful. Another possibility is that as children these then non-Catholics were influenced by the very strong institutional Catholic socialization of their childhood friends or relatives.

Finally, in the sociology of conversion literature, "the socialization hypothesis" assumes that the transmission of religious values is related to social climate. When religion is favored, transmission of religious activity and belief will be strongest (McAllister, 1988:259). The experience of the older new Catholics in this study suggests that social climates where religion was not favored in their past are not impediments to accepting religious belief and activity in the present. Remembering the disfavor of religion in one's household or childhood seems to translate into a stronger motivation to become Catholic in the present. For these older new Catholics, then, the past is re-socialized. The social realities of the present are related to the social realities of the past, particularly early childhood. A social reconstruction is operative.[13]

Prayer Group Members and Early Childhood Memories

Among the lifelong Catholics of the prayer group early childhood memories were prominent as well. Reflections on childhood were explicitly encouraged. For example, at one prayer group meeting a prepared prayer was read by Sister Agnes. The prayer said, "O God of young faith and new beginnings, I remember the church of my childhood where you first stepped into my life and gave me your life." Karen responded saying, "Isn't that so true?" Joan then described the church of her childhood.

In our interview, Karen recalled the struggles of growing up Catholic in a Protestant neighborhood in Scotland. Her words reflected the importance of Roman Catholicism in her past, and its continued importance today. Karen is discontented with many of the changes in the Catholic Church. She used to find comfort in the teaching that the Catholic Church was the "one true" church. She feels this is no longer the case. She stated:

> Now I feel like I am one of the herd. I mean, I'm the same as the Baptists, the Methodists, and I don't like that feeling. I want to be the other. That might be just because I am growing old and I am not accepting the fact that I am old. Maybe my mind is reverting. It leaves me dissatisfied. That's another reason why I enjoy going to the little prayer group meeting with Sister; we have the time to sit down and to analyze. I have an open mind about religion. I love my own. I like what it was. And I'm not terribly happy with what it is. And, again, as I say, with you, and the young people coming into the church in their thirties, you're in a different world.

Ironically, St. Anthony's, a church many consider to be progressive, provides a specific context for Karen's life review. It is not simply the Catholic Church that appeals to her, it is the traditional Catholic Church that proclaims the Christ she grew up with. The Catholic Church of her memory is the frame for her review. St. Anthony's reminds her of the church of her memories. Karen's words are more convincing: "There was something about St. Anthony's. Plus, I don't really go for modern churches. I mean the Christ I pray to is the Christ I grew up with. I don't like these square faces [square faces of Christ in modern art]. I find it hard to pray in modern churches." Karen summarized her reflections with her motto statement, "Yes, I am really still what I was."

Sister Agnes's own experience with dealing with painful childhood memories provided a context in which discussing the past, and early childhood, was viewed as important. Agnes' mother died when Agnes was twelve years old. As a teenager Agnes was placed in various foster homes and boarding schools. She did not feel wanted. Her memories of childhood were so "incorrigible," to use her description, that she sought the counsel of a psychiatrist about a decade ago. Agnes stated, "I used to be ashamed to talk about my life. People would ask me about my family and I would say 'You don't want to hear about it; it sounds like a soap opera.'" She decided to go to a psychiatrist especially to deal with childhood memories. She credited her two years of therapy for giving her a new freedom to talk about her past. "He [the psychiatrist] said, 'Why would you not talk about it? That's what brought you to what you are.' So I got over that." Agnes said that she would not change anything in her life if it meant changing the person she is today. Her grappling with early childhood memories was reflected in an openness to such topics in the prayer group.

Paula has the final perspective on the importance of early childhood memories in later life:

Do you find yourself looking back much on your life?

Yes. And also annoyed when I do so. Because I sometimes—A few days ago I was getting breakfast and my mind was way back. I had remembered something and I thought, That's interesting; I never knew that. And I was intent on it. I discovered my coffee in my cereal!

[both laughing] *Oh, no!*

And two or three things like that. And then I thought, No wonder my mind is way back here when I was possibly eight or nine years old. There is—I read somewhere—I used to read a great deal of psychiatry, and they tell us that in later years it—people invariably go back to their childhood because that is the beginning. You try to think this is the way it was when I began and on through the years. So my memory of things way, way back there is much clearer than the day before yesterday. And as I said, it annoys me. But that's the way it is.

Early Childhood Memories Summary

Both the newcomers to Roman Catholicism and the lifelong Catholics found in their respective social groups an arena for discussing and confronting early childhood memories. The RCIA participants did indicate more of a propensity to reconstruct their childhood memories, whereas the prayer group members discussed their past more in terms of progress, development, and an integrated life story. Once again, both the RCIA participants and the prayer group members found their early childhood memories directly affecting the decisions they made regarding religious practice and belonging.

Berger and Luckmann's perspective serves as an apt summary of the influence of early childhood memories among both groups:

> The world of childhood is so constituted as to instill in the individual a nomic structure in which he may have confidence that "everything is all right." ...The discovery that some things are far from "all right" may be more or less shocking, depending on biographical circumstances, but in either case the world of childhood is likely to retain its peculiar reality in retrospection. It remains the "home world," however far one may travel from it in later life into regions where one does not feel at home at all (1967:136).

CONCLUSION

Throughout this chapter we have examined the interaction of personal and social aspects of the RCIA. The stories that individuals told about becoming Catholic were both combative, such as Cathy's, and complacent in nature, such as Clara's. This interaction is summarized well in the words of an RCIA professional:

> At all stages in the process we invite inquirers to see themselves not as passive receivers but as active participants in their own

story now, and later, if they choose, in the stories and life of their fellow travelers in both Church and world (Dunning, 1981b:184).

In this chapter we have witnessed the autonomy of the individual as the individual uses the social structure of the Catholic Church in facing issues of age, in answering questions of meaning, in responding to the challenges of life crises and transitions, and in grappling with the task of integration posed by early childhood memories. The older new Catholics are not simply "products" of the social influence of the RCIA, they also deliberately effect change in their lives through the RCIA process. In chapter 4, the focus is placed on the power and presence of significant others and the social structure of the RCIA.

Notes

1. Despite the clear life-review aspects of Ben's story, he seemed to indicate his family was primary in his becoming Catholic. He said his wife "almost fell in a faint" when he told her he wanted to become Catholic. Yet when I asked him, "Well, say, if your wife weren't Catholic, do you think you would be Catholic today?" he replied, "I don't think so, Father, unless—She has a big influence on me. If she was in her religion, I woulda probably went that way too, different, y'know, to keep her and the children and us all happy going to one church, where it makes us all one big group; do you know what I'm sayin'?" Thus Ben is another example of an individual who clearly indicated a variety of motivating factors in becoming Catholic, including a religious conversion experience, the life review, and family influence. Mixed into the dynamics of Ben's becoming Catholic is the fact that some of his considerations were prompted by his age.

2. The feeling of security Judy mentioned predates the RCIA process. Paula, the member of the prayer group who became Catholic in later life, when asked what it meant for her to be Catholic, named "the inner feelings, a deep feeling of security." Karen, another prayer group member, described "my religion" as "a covering, it's a cloak, it's something that is very important to me. If it was taken away from me, what would I have? I wouldn't have anything."

3. The sense of security Judy found, and its rootedness in the meaning it conveys, is echoed in Clara's words, "If I didn't believe in God and I didn't have prayer, I don't know what I would do, seriously."

4. When Reverend Jones spoke of the "real presence" he was referring to a belief that distinguishes Catholicism from most Protestant denominations. Catholicism teaches that Jesus Christ is "really present" in the bread and wine, whereas most Protestant denominations teach that the bread and wine are

symbols of Jesus' presence.

5. Reverend Jones' story cannot be told by simply and solely suggesting he was an active religious seeker. His memory of his love for a Catholic girl continues to be a powerful force in his life. When I asked him if there were things in life he would do differently he said he would have married the Catholic girl and "just not think about" the protests of his parents because she was Catholic. He said he had a happy life with his wife: "God did provide and I did get a wonderful wife and family, but I still realize that I was in love very much, the kind of love that doesn't come too often."

Additionally, as the section below indicates, Reverend Jones became Catholic at a traumatic time in his life. Also, Reverend Jones spoke of his Irish heritage: "It's an anomaly to be an Irishman and not be Roman Catholic." When I asked him what he found appealing about his parish, he replied, "I like everything about the church. I especially enjoy all the Irish in there...." The attraction of the Irish individuals and heritage for Reverend Jones supports Berger and Luckmann's discussion of the importance of analyzing the "macroscopic social roots of a religious world view" and "the manner in which this world view is manifested in the consciousness of an individual" (1967:79). Berger and Luckmann specifically mention ethnic groups as an example of the macroscopic social roots.

Thus Reverend Jones is another example of an individual for whom a monocausal theory of membership shift would not be adequate. In his story Reverend Jones mentions the influence of family, significant others, religious experience, feeling at home, doctrinal issues, solidarity with the Irish, and transition in his life. His experience speaks not only against a monocausal theory of religious conversion or membership switching, but also against labeling any one factor as solely important in an individual's effort to reconstruct his/her personal or social world.

6. The movement Clara describes here is exemplary of Berger and Luckmann's discussion of externalization, objectification, and internalization (1967:129).

7. Yet, when Clara was asked, "What attracted you to Roman Catholicism as opposed to any other religion?" she replied in a matter-of-fact fashion: "Just because I went to church all the time with my husband." Early in the interview she emphasized the importance of family harmony; later in the interview she said, "I never did feel there should be friction in a family over religion...." Clara is another example of an individual strongly identifying a number of motivating factors for becoming Catholic.

8. The relevance of crisis situations for religious conversion has been debated in literature. For example, Parrucci's theoretical analysis results in the claim, "To the extent that the individual perceives these situations to be stressful and defines his problem from a religious problem-solving perspective,

his reaction will take the form of religious conversion" (1968:150). Heirich, on the other hand, calling on his comparison group data, suggests stress is inadequate to account for religious conversions (1977:666).

9. A psychotherapist would not be surprised at the role of early childhood memories in the lives of older adults. Freud devoted much of his effort to understanding the means by which early childhood memories are represented in adult life (Cohler, 1982:216). Erik Erikson drew parallels between early and later life citing the significance each stage had for the other (Erikson, 1982:62).

10. Cathy experienced both an elective affinity with Roman Catholicism and an intentional use of Roman Catholic membership to combat early childhood memories. For Cathy, prominence was given to her individual experience in the dialectic between the individual and the social structure.

11. Deb's words reflect Berger and Luckmann's discussion of the link between childhood and later life in subjective reality. They state, "Socialization in later life typically begins to take on an affectivity reminiscent of childhood when it seeks radically to transform the subjective reality of the individual" (1967:141).

12. For a discussion of the relationship of religious conversions with biological fathers, see Chana Ullman's study of the psychology of religious conversion. Ullman suggests "the father problem," that is, early childhood trauma relating to fathers, "plays an important role" in religious conversion (1989:44–45).

13. Roof and Hoge cite Catholic childhood socialization as a strong independent influence in church involvement in later years. Such a strong independent influence of socialization is not found among Protestants in Roof and Hoge's sample (1980:423).

4
Family Influence and Sense of Belonging

The influence of significant others is constantly cited as one of the prime influences in religious conversion literature. This chapter examines the influence of significant others within the family structure and within the social structure of the Catholic Church. Chapter 3 focused on the efforts of the RCIA participants to make sense of their experience and find meaning. This chapter focuses on the meaning and sense that is provided by the family and the church.

FAMILY INFLUENCE

Family influence is a significant factor in the decision to become Catholic among the RCIA participants.[1] Indeed, the influence of one's spouse or one's children is the factor most often cited by the older new Catholics in prompting their decision to join the Catholic Church. Their stories are often not only of becoming Catholic, but also of an effort to become a unified couple, or a unified family.

John, the man whose son died suddenly, answered the question, "So could you tell me how you happened to become Catholic?" in this way: "Well, I can only blame one person, and give her the credit; she [wife] went through the RCIA." John's explanation for his becoming Catholic was very simple: "My wife has always been the number one thing for me…so really the main reason I became Catholic is because she did."

Pierre credited his children with prompting his decision to become Catholic:

And so my two children were confirmed. And so I was sittin' in the church while they were goin' out and taking the—the wine and the food, Christ. And I was just sitting there and I says, "This is not right; we gotta complete the family in one direction."

Independence of Decision Upheld

Even those for whom spousal and familial influence was a strong factor in becoming Catholic, the independence of their decision was upheld. A constant refrain in our interviews was that the spouses or family members did not "push" or even suggest that their loved ones become Catholic. Lenny, the Jewish-to-Catholic man, spoke of his wife's surprise when he decided to become Catholic after forty years of marriage: "No time in that forty years did Karen even suggest remotely that possibly I could convert, possibly, you know. In fact, she was very surprised when I went to the RCIA program." Joan told a similar story of her Catholic male companion of thirty-eight years: "Carl never asked me at all to become a Catholic, never. We were friends for thirty-eight years; not one time did he ever ask me." Willard one day announced to his wife that he would accompany her to church after she had gone alone for forty years: "She just about dropped her teeth." Judy said about her husband, "Paddy did not encourage me or say, 'I want you to become a Catholic.' He never did say that to me. He didn't force me into it at all. It was my own, totally my own decision. Nobody told me I should do this." Even John, who above gave the credit (and blame) to his wife for his becoming Catholic, said about his wife, "She didn't say anything, she was great, good about it, not kind of pushy."

Clara emphasized the independence that others upheld in speaking of her husband and in-laws: "They never put pressure on me and that makes a big difference because then you can make up your own mind and you don't feel that you're pushed into something."

Despite the constant claim of independence from family influence in decision-making, spousal influence was acknowledged in some cases. Pierre's wife served as his sponsor. When I asked him, "What role did your wife play as your sponsor?" he detailed her direct influence:

She was one that got me to every meeting when I would say, "Oh, gee, I don't know, dear. I think I'll skip this one." [Chuckle] She says,

"No, you're going. You obligated yourself; you go through the course. You can't be like that." So then, after I got started, I said, "I love this; it's the way to go."

Of the twenty-eight new Catholics, five were sponsored by their spouses (an additional woman had her husband as her godfather, which is a more limited role), one was sponsored by his brother-in-law, and three were sponsored by their daughters. For these ten individuals the independence of their family members in the RCIA process would, at least, be confounded by their taking an active role in supporting the process of becoming Catholic.

Willard surprised me at the end of our interview. He spoke during the interview of his close relationship with God, of having a vision of Jesus while in battle, of God saving his wife from cancer, and of the friendliness, love and acceptance he found in his parish which he called "the greatest parish in the world." When I asked him, "How has your family reacted to your becoming Catholic?" he replied with laughter and conviction, "Personally, I don't care." About his wife he said, "I was married to Cathy, but I wouldn't say that was an influence on my becoming Catholic." And, "We never used religion, y'know, for or against one another." Yet in the final words of our interview he revealed the core of his decision to become Catholic, saying, "I think the most important thing, the satisfying thing is I made my wife really, really happy. I mean, she never pushed or anything like that. I am happy for her because finally it sunk into my thick head." What is surprising about this statement is that throughout our interview so many other motivational factors seemed to be active in his story. Whether or not his wife being Catholic was *the* reason Willard became Catholic, still, for him, the bottom line was that his membership in the Catholic Church made her happy.

The influence of interfaith marriages is addressed by Berger and Luckmann. They emphasize the importance of a spouse as a significant other. "A reality-disconfirming act by the wife, taken by itself, has far greater potency than a similar act by a casual acquaintance" (1967:151). Berger and Luckmann illustrate this point saying, "If one is a believing Catholic the reality of one's faith need not be threatened by non-believing business associates. It is very likely to be threatened, however, by a non-believing wife" (1967:152).

Spousal influence also worked in another direction. Two new

Catholics said their joining the Catholic Church had brought their husbands back to church. Both husbands were non-participating Catholics. Maureen suggested her husband was a "major hurdle" to overcome: He fought: "You're not going tonight."..."You're not doing that."..."You're not feeling well."..."I don't want you to become too churchy."

For some individuals, family influence was still evident but in a secondary way. After attending church with a spouse or children for many years, these people gradually desired full membership and full participation in the Catholic Church. A frequently told story among these new Catholics was regular church attendance for twenty-five to forty years. Later in life the desire to be a full member, and to move from being an "outsider" to a member, was expressed. In Berger and Luckmann's terms, what these people came to "know" as reality in their everyday lives was weekly church attendance. This reality was continually affirmed in their interactions with others, particularly in interaction with their spouses and children. The objective reality they participated in on a weekly basis was socially defined by a church which emphasized full membership. Their individual consciousness was socially determined (1967:78). Membership in the church became dominatingly plausible.[2]

An additional insight from Berger and Luckmann, which relates to those individuals who attended church for many years as non-members, is what the authors call a "meaningful reciprocity in processes of institutionalization" (1967:64). Berger and Luckmann explain this concept: "As the individual reflects about the successive moments of his experience, he tries to fit their meanings into a consistent biographical framework; this tendency increases as the individual shares with others his meanings and their biographical integration" (1967:64).

Given the reciprocity in processes of institutionalization, what is surprising about the stories the new Catholics tell is not that they joined the Church after twenty-five to forty years of regular attendance. Rather, what is surprising is that it took twenty-five to forty years to join.

Finally, in discussing specific plausibility structures, Berger and Luckmann cite as an example, "One can maintain one's Catholic faith only if one retains one's significant relationship with the Catholic community…" (1967:155). The experiences of the people in this study add the fact that one can only become a Catholic if one has a significant relationship with the Catholic community, even if the "community" is embodied in one individual (the spouse).

The Reception of Communion and Family Unity

The reception of communion, which is reserved for full members of the church in good standing, is a powerful motivator and symbol of membership. One woman wanted to know, "When I was going through RCIA I was not allowed to receive communion. Why?" Jim spoke of attending church for twenty-five years with his wife, "but I was never Catholic. Everybody'd get up to go to communion and I sat there, and they hobbled over me and around me and so forth." Once he could receive communion he "became Catholic," despite twenty-five years of attending the church. One husband told me of what he called a "symbolic act." He had discontinued his own reception of communion until his wife became a full member and could receive her communion.

Fred, an eighty-one-year-old man, spoke frequently in our interview about his love affair with his wife of over fifty years. He captured the dual influence of attending with his wife and not being able to receive communion in his answer to the question, "Now, was there a particular reason why you did it [became Catholic] at that time in your life?"

> Well, I guess—I guess I thought that it was about time. The big thing that was missing in my going to church with Grace was…when she would get up and leave me sitting there and she would go to communion, and I felt—That's when I felt, well, I'm just not a part of this at all, and I wanted to be a part of it, particularly with Grace; I wanted this to be something that she and I had in common.

Perceived Church Teaching and Family Life

The benefits that the older new Catholics perceive to family life in Catholicism are also reflected in their perceptions of church teaching. Helen thought that if she had been a practicing Catholic previously her first marriage might have been saved. Her attitude was reflected in her answer to the question, "What Catholic beliefs are appealing to you?"

> Well, I think that one of the things is staying together, working things out; I think that's very important. Not jumping at divorce just because you don't—something doesn't—And I think that—I think that's very important, staying together with family and raising the family together. I think that—communicating with each other; I think that's very, very important. It makes a better grounds for better home life and for the young people growing up. I think that's very important. But I think that's one of the things that the Catholic religion does: it focuses on family and on home, from the little ones on up.

I am surprised that intermarriage is such a prominent factor in the stories I have been told. Since the people whom I interviewed were not newly married I expected the issues posed by diverse religious practices to be addressed, one way or another, earlier in married life. Yet the interfaith aspects of marriage are a significant factor even for those who have been married for over forty years. For many in this study they are not only reconstructing their biographies, they are reconstructing their family lives. They construct and reconstruct their families based on a vision of familial solidarity they perceive the church to teach.

One of the most prominent models in sociology of religious conversion research is Lofland and Stark's theory of conversion to a deviant perspective (1965). For many of the older new Catholics, they were converting *from* a deviant perspective. As the only member in a family who was not Catholic, or as one of the few individuals who attended Catholic services regularly without being a member, these individuals held a deviant perspective. By becoming members of the Catholic Church, they were removing that deviant perspective.

Family Obstacles to Becoming Catholic

The family role in the process of becoming Catholic for the older new Catholics comes not only from those who support membership in the church, it also comes in the removal of often long-standing family obstacles to becoming Catholic. Ida told of her first husband being offended when a priest visited their home and said, "We are not interested in your wife, but we want to get you back to church." Ida said, "Well, that did it!" Her husband told her, "Don't you ever talk to me again about going back to church." As soon as her husband died, she contacted a Catholic church to seek membership. Becoming

Catholic was so important in Ida's life that she delayed chemotherapy treatments for lymphoma until after she became a member of the church because she felt the treatments would make her "have to come out of RCIA...." Her husband's protest could keep her from becoming Catholic, but cancer would not.

Deb spoke of her father's ardent anti-Catholicism. Even though her mother was a Catholic, Deb was raised in the Episcopal Church. When I suggested it was "unusual" for her to be raised Episcopal, Deb replied, "My father wouldn't allow us to go anyplace near a Catholic church. We couldn't even talk about it; it was a forbidden subject."

Some people joined the church even in the face of opposition from their families. Gloria said, "A lot of people in my family don't approve of it at all," and "Well, my son, who is not Catholic, he was very annoyed with me." Gloria would have images of her dead mother protesting her joining the Catholic faith.[3] Additionally, Gloria said her sister was so anti-Catholic that "I knew that I could never take this step while she was alive because she'd have a fit."

Becoming Catholic as a Threat to Family Accord

Joining a spouse in religious affiliation does not necessarily add to marital accord. Judy told of tension in her relationship with her husband based on differences in religious approach. She married her husband late in life.

> I told my husband—He wanted me at first to say the rosary every day with him, out loud. I didn't feel comfortable doing that. And I felt like I was maybe being hypocritical in a way because I didn't feel like I was doing something that I wanted to do on my own volition. So I—One day I said to him, "No, I am not going to do it anymore. I'll say the rosary when I feel like it and when I want to. But to be forced to do it, I don't feel comfortable with it." So he got quite upset about it, but he accepted it. I said, "You know, Paddy, before I married you, you accepted me as I was, the person that I was. So my personal life, and religion in a way...is my own, as long as I do what the Church requires: I go to church, I go on holy days of obligation, and I try to be charitable to people, and I try to...do the right thing in all things."

The strong social cohesion (discussed below) that develops in most RCIA groups poses threats to family solidarity. People told me of their spouses' concerns that they were getting too religious or spending too much time at the church. For some the RCIA group became a pseudo-family or additional family:

> But anyhow, these people were so nice, so friendly, so genuine, there wasn't a phony bone or statement from any of 'em, and we all became like a family. We all became very close, and we all shared the experience. It was wonderful! It was—I had never dreamt that such a thing could happen.

Jim added, "My wife gets a little upset sometimes because I guess she never experienced that type of a relationship." Finally, Jim said, "It wasn't planned; it just happened." Yet in some ways the notion of the RCIA group as another family *is* planned. The church is described and compared to a family. For example, in an RCIA handbook, the small group leader is told to:

> Give examples of commitments families must make due to illness in the family, a disabled member of the family, the loss of a job, the building of a new house or the need to welcome an aging in-law. Ask the group to share ideas of such common family commitments. Compare these incidents to the commitment made by the community, whereby they must work together for the sake of the catechumens (Anderson, 1986:27).

Despite the mention of family in this handbook, what is most striking in my field observations is the lack of attention given to the newcomers' families. There are occasional expressions of concern for family members or religious tension in a family. Family members may be welcomed at the meetings or at RCIA social functions. But, by and large, the candidate is approached in isolation from his/her familial context (O'Rourke, 1987: 17).[4]

Family Life in the Prayer Group

The nature of family interaction is not easily comparable in considering the similarities and differences of the new Catholics with the prayer group members. Family concerns were a very prominent issue in prayer group meetings and in our interviews. Concerns for close and distant relatives were often expressed. All members of the prayer group lived alone. Daily interaction with family members was limited to telephone calls.

One member had met her husband at a Catholic church and had a priest and church cook as their best man and maid of honor. Another member's husband had converted to Catholicism. At one meeting one of the members said that in the prayer group she could talk about things that she didn't talk to anyone else about, "like our family." Furthermore, the things they talked about in the group would be a "burden" to their children. Thus the prayer group, similar to the RCIA groups, served as a pseudo-family.

One distinction which is clear is that the new Catholics describe their family as being first in importance in their lives. Family influence, in many cases, appears primary to religious influences. For the prayer group members, God and religion were first. Joan stated this fact succinctly: "Well, my family and my God are what is important to me. My God first; then my family." I asked, "Has it always been that way?" Joan answered, "Yes, I've always...tried to put God first. And I'd tell my children, 'Put God first and everything else will follow.'" Darleen said, "Anything pertaining to the church always means so much to me. It comes first in my life."

Family Influences Summary

Family dynamics are important to recognize in the motivation to change religions, in the removal of long-standing familial religious objections, in the threat to family solidarity that the social cohesion of RCIA groups may pose, and in the comparisons with individuals for whom religion has been important over the long term. Berger and Luckmann emphasize the dual influences of significant others and reference groups. For many older new Catholics in this study, their spouses or children were the "significant others" and their family unit was the primary reference group. They at once sought to change the family unit and were influenced by the social realities of the family.

SENSE OF BELONGING

A frequent theme among the new Catholics was a renewed sense of belonging that resulted from joining the church. By belonging to the church, they discovered new meanings for their lives and new personal identities. The desire to belong was a motivation to join the church.

Identity and Belonging

When one woman was asked, "What does it mean to you now to be a Catholic?" she replied, "It has strengthened and revived my faith. It means that I belong somewhere in God's family." Lenny attended with his wife for forty years; in the year before joining the RCIA he attended *daily* mass and daily publicly prayed the rosary. The percentage of Catholic Americans who engage in both activities on a daily basis is minuscule. Yet, for Lenny, the initiation ceremonies and welcoming were needed so that he could say, "Hey, now I'm truly a member, y'know. And I'm being welcomed by all these people!" One woman discussed how being Catholic, "Makes me the proudest person in the world." In fact, she suggested, "I keep saying I want to go to the hospital so I can put down that I am Catholic."

Berger and Luckmann state, "Identity is ultimately legitimated by placing it within the context of a symbolic universe" (1967:100). Gloria expressed a clear endorsement of this notion. She proclaimed, "I am an enriched person, belonging." Explaining this statement, she said, "When you join the Catholic religion, you feel you have an identity with something...." Finally, she concluded, "And when you grow up in a big city, it's my firm belief that you have to have an identity with a group. And I think that is a great way to face up to taking religion on too." Later in our interview Gloria emphasized this perspective: "You need to have a church where you can actually go, and not just go to the mass. We need to have a feeling of belonging to the parish...."[5]

Berger and Luckmann place in theoretical perspective the link that Gloria draws in her experience between identity and belonging. "A meaningful universe" is both a source of identity and a motivation for belonging (1967:103). Gloria personifies Berger and Luckmann's claim that "identity is formed by social processes" (1967:173).

The social recognition of a new identity was evident in a regional liturgy I attended to welcome new Catholics. During the mass the deacon prayed for the new Catholics, "For all those among us who are neophytes, and neophytes throughout the church, that they continue to learn who you really are, that you are Christ the Lord." Now that they are new Catholics, they are discovering who they "really are."

Although the Catholic Church does not prohibit contact with "the outside world," as do many cults and sects (Kilbourne and Richardson, 1989:12), RCIA directors and teams are encouraged to foster the sense of belonging. An RCIA handbook gives the following instruction to the small-group leader:

> Share an experience of your own need to belong to some group or some person, and what you did about it. Ask the group to share their experiences. How were you received, and how did you feel about the way others were willing to receive or not receive you? Relate how the catechumens now express their desire to belong, and try to point out the important role of the community which commits itself to the catechumen (Anderson, 1986:26).

Appeal of Additional Social Involvement and of Catholic People

The strength of the need for a sense of belonging as a motivator for older people to join the Catholic Church was evident when I asked the question, "At the time you began the RCIA process, was added social involvement pleasing to you?" The vast majority of the new Catholics replied affirmatively. This overwhelming affirmation of added social involvement surprised me. When I asked the participants if they would be Catholic today if not for the influence of some significant other they mentioned, many indicated perhaps not, but the significant other was not *the reason* they became Catholic. For example, one man described the personal influence of a priest in his decision to become Catholic. I asked him, "Do you think you'd be Catholic today if it weren't for his influence?" He responded:

> Well, I really can't answer that. To tell the truth, I would hate to believe that that would be true. I mean, I would hate to believe that my becoming a Catholic was dependent upon one priest. That doesn't appeal to me.

If this line of thought was followed in the "social involvement" question, the new Catholics would have answered that social involvement was pleasing to them but not *the reason* to join the church. Instead, they mainly answered this question in an unqualified affirmative response. Liza, as an example, said simply, "I wanted to meet more people who were concerned about growing spiritually...so I was looking for some kind of community."

The wife of one man underlined the social value of the RCIA:

> When our children were growing up and going to the parochial schools...I was naturally involved in the Mothers' Club and everything, so it was very easy to become a member of the congregation socially. So we were involved over there socially. After your children are out of school, and as you get older, it's difficult going into a new parish, it's difficult to make social contacts, and RCIA was one way we did it....

In another woman's words we see that in addition to personal biography and family, often social worlds and social interactions are reconstructed. Ida said, "All of our friends are of this parish....And, you know, anything that the church has we participate in—any activities." Ida's use of the words "all" and "any" indicates the all-inclusive social nature of the church in her and her husband's life since she joined the church. Ida's socialization appears to be more with the RCIA group than with the church community. When she attends mass she still sits in the RCIA section even though she has "graduated" from the process. She does so because she knows the RCIA leader and the people in that section are "friendly and warm." For many of the new Catholics, the RCIA became a focal point of social integration and activity in their lives.

The view of RCIA people or Catholics as happy, peaceful, or holy people was frequently mentioned in our interviews. Lula stated, "There seems that there is a special happiness that Catholics have; it's in their face, it's in their stature, it's the way they walk or talk or whatever. It's there." Sally explained it this way: Her Catholic friends throughout her life, "always seemed to have such a different attitude, different feeling towards life than a lot of people."

Reverend Jones spoke of a woman he had loved early in his life. Since his wife has died, he is planning to marry this woman he still calls "a Catholic girl":

> She's still alive and so we're gonna get married one of these days. But I think she started me off on that [Catholicism], just the purity of her own life, the respect I had for her. And I was wondering, what is it about Catholicism that, y'know, is so different from Methodism?

Ironically, members of the prayer group spoke often about the special nature of converts, particularly when referring to Paula. Paula spoke of envying "cradle Catholics," whereas the cradle Catholics spoke of envying Paula as a convert. Joan's words about converts were very similar to the new Catholics' perceptions about cradle Catholics:

> Oh, the Catholic faith, there is nothing like it! It's—It's—you know. I think a born Catholic, a person who is born in the religion, I don't think we appreciate our religion as much as a convert. Because I have several friends who are converts. And they are—I'm sure they are better people than I am. They seem to know the Bible backwards and forwards, and they go to church every day. They are very reverent. And it's like, when you talk about religion, their face shines, and such a glow comes over their face.

The movement from attraction to a significant other to attraction to Roman Catholicism among the RCIA participants is also evident in Larry's recollection of a man who influenced him at age eleven:

> Working as a box boy in—During high school there was a guy by the name of Frederick and he was Catholic. And they did not know this at first, but I liked this guy. He was just a really, really nice person. And I told my mother when I was in high school, "You know, I think I am going to become a Catholic." And she said, "WHAT! [laughing] How did you decide that?" I said, "Well, there is this fellow down at work and I just like him; I mean, he seems to have it, you know, everything. He's just a really nice person." "Well, you know you shouldn't just base it on that." So I didn't make the move then, but I was really impressed with this man; I still am. I think he is just a beautiful human being.

Peg suggested that both people and the churches contribute to a feeling of holiness in Catholicism:

> *What attracted you to Catholicism as opposed to any other religion?*
>
> You mean as opposed to any other? I've always thought that Catholicism was basically more of a solemn—I don't know how to put it—presence; you feel the presence of God more I think in a cathedral or church or I don't know what the word is. Holy!

> *Mm-hum.*
>
> It's a good word....I'm sure that—that the other Christians wouldn't think that, but I'm sure I feel it; I feel it more.

Dave also underlined the unique approach of Roman Catholicism as he compared "fellowship" in his experience of Protestantism with the notion of fellowship in the Catholic Church:

> When I go to mass there's always somebody to come up and hug them that we helped or helped us. That's comforting; that's nice—that sense of belonging; that sense of—We've got something that's right, and people recognize that. And so there—there is a—there's a fellowship that I think is based on the worship and…the love of God that comes from Catholicism as opposed to having fellowship or—because we're together.

Thus the uniqueness of Catholics as a group, and the way that uniqueness showed in its members, its places, and its method of worship was appealing to many of the older new Catholics when they considered joining the church. As they sought to make sense of their world, they saw in Catholics as individuals, and in Catholicism as a religion, a uniqueness and sense of well-being that was attractive.

For some people the social attraction of the RCIA, and its members, was the primary motivating factor. Some of these individuals approached the church with an attitude similar to Weber's notion of status groups, whereby motivation for church membership is similar to motivation for involvement in lodges or country clubs. That is, there is an identity and honor in membership, a full social life, and a common lifestyle (Weber,1946: 186; Roof and Hoge, 1980:424). A clear example of a status group mentality was demonstrated by one man's asking the man he sponsored in the Elks to be his sponsor in the church.

The RCIA as a Powerful Social Force

Perhaps most important in considering the social aspects of membership and socialization, the RCIA process is a powerful social force. This force is especially evident in the emphasis on small groups. Berger and Luckmann suggest that the "face-to-face situation…is the prototypical case of social interaction" (1967:28). The reality of everyday life is shared with others, and the face-to-face situation is a powerful expression of the reality of everyday life. The face-to-face nature of the small-group interaction in the RCIA process has definitive attraction and reality molding impact on the participants.

The influence of one's relevance structure (Berger and Luckmann, 1967:45) on another individual was recognized in the interviews and in field observations. One RCIA coordinator told me about one of the men in the RCIA group: "I was working on him for four years." This statement implies personal influence in seeking new members for the Catholic Church. A RCIA participant told me, "Well, I talked one gal into joining it [RCIA]."

The social strength of the group approach of the RCIA is evident in Maureen's description of how she became Catholic:

> So the last time I was in the hospital, which was about—it was about two and a half years ago. And I signed in; when I put religious preference, I put "Catholic." I didn't know what else to. It was better than putting a question mark. So Father Jim came over to see me, and Sister Mary, and I explained that I wasn't Catholic, but they were very gracious with me and kept coming back. And a man named John came in and talked to me and said, "You know, you might be interested in the RCIA group....I'll tell you, why don't you call Sister Ruth?" So, instead, he gave Sister Ruth my name, and once you get on Sister Ruth's list...[intonation and expression indicates Sister Ruth was persistent]. So she called me. And I was recovering and I couldn't go out of the house, and she just kept inviting me and calling to see how I was, and when I was well enough I went to a meeting, and I was literally hooked. I didn't know whether to become a Catholic, but I didn't want to leave that group.

Notice that Maureen does not remember the visitor saying you might be interested "in the RCIA"; rather, she remembers "the RCIA *group*." The group was the primary focus of Maureen's experience of becoming a Catholic. Maureen said she never made a decision to become Catholic. Similar to getting married, "being a Catholic wasn't a decision I ever had to make."[6] Additionally, because of the step-by-step nature of the rites in the RCIA, Maureen said, "I just seemed to be ready for each one. I guess I never made a decision."[7]

The step-by-step nature of the RCIA process that Maureen

described is a gradual means of socialization. Berger and Luckmann draw a parallel conclusion in discussing the socialization of religious personnel. Such socialization typically involves "the institutionalization of an elaborate initiation process, a novitiate, in the course of which the individual comes to commit himself fully to the reality that is being internalized"(1967:145).[8] The gradual commitments required by RCIA participants at definite steps in the process add to the power of socialization.

When I asked Maureen what "hooked" her about the RCIA group, she said, "The love, absolute love and acceptance. You see, I always am looking for acceptance, right?" Maureen described the RCIA as at first informative, but later as "a support group." An example of the social binding of individuals as a support group comes from Maureen's description of a discontented member of the group. One of the class members was told by the team that the team felt she was motivated by her fiance and should reconsider joining the church. When she came to complain to Maureen, Maureen's reaction was, "I guess what I felt then was defensive of the group, because when she talked to me my experience had been so different."[9]

Maureen's experience of the social force of the group was echoed by Jim, who spoke of being "won over" by the group:

> I think the RCIA is such a winner because when you go in there, you're not considered a convert. When you go in there, they're just looking you over and you're lookin' them over; it's inquiry—it absolutely is inquiry. So you have a chance to let it all hang out, to ask your questions and listen to their answers and kinda figure, Well, how does their answer compare to the ones that you heard in the past? Which one makes the most sense? Which has more logic? And I think they will win you over—I really do; I think Catholic—the theory and practice of Catholicism is strong enough in its own to win people over, to win converts. And I think the RCIA does a great job.

In this paragraph Jim puts into words the notion of Berger and Luckmann, as derived from Schutz, that, "My interaction with others in everyday life is, therefore, constantly affected by our common participation in the available social stock of knowledge" (1967:41). For Jim, the dual benefits of the RCIA came in his interaction with others and the ways in which the "social stock of knowledge" incorporated in the RCIA helped him make sense of his reality.

Additionally, in the quotation above, Jim mentioned the desirability of entering the process as an inquirer and not as a convert. Many people found the initial role of an inquirer to be desirable. They felt less commitment and therefore less pressure. If, as Neugarten and Datan suggest, "The success of the socialization process is measured by the ability of the individual to perform well in the roles he takes on" (1973:56), then the RCIA is a successful socialization process. The role of inquirer is one that was appealing and easily adopted by the RCIA participants.

The informal approach to the inquiry stage was evident in the way the rooms for meetings were set up in one parish I visited. On the same evening, in two adjacent rooms, the new inquirers and the veteran catechumens met. At the catechumen meeting the participants faced a podium sitting on chairs set up in rows. At the new inquirers meeting chairs were set up in a circle. There was no podium; the leader for the meeting sat in the circle as opposed to standing at the podium.

Despite the effort at informality, "all institutionalized conduct involves roles" (Berger and Luckmann, 1967: 74). By playing the role of the inquirer, the individual participates in the social world of Roman Catholicism. And, in Berger and Luckmann's words, by internalizing this role the same world "becomes subjectively real to him" (1967:74).[10]

Some Negative Social Experiences

Gloria discussed some negative reactions to the social nature of the process. She said, "I met certainly lovely people there, but that [social involvement] was not…one of the benefits." Gloria implied that the group may actually have been stifling religious experience or expression. She indicated she felt more religious in her life after she went through the RCIA process:

> I think that probably it [religiosity] was sort of a build-up during the program and then afterwards when you start practicing on your own and not just going to the class, it became more meaningful because we went to the mass only as a group, and then we left, you know, before the communion. So I think it was probably more satisfying after it was finished.

Pierre spoke of younger people who, in his view, should have stayed in the process longer. He did so in a way that may have shown a jealousy that they did not follow group procedures:

> I saw some faults from a couple of people that were leaving the group....I figured it was going to happen since they didn't go through the group; they kinda pushed them through very quickly without thinking of the long-term effect on these two people.

Betty was one of the most engaging persons I met. Her energy and her vibrant vocabulary were leveled against the RCIA. She had a history of bad experiences with the Catholic Church, beginning when the priest in her home town refused to baptize her because she had been born to an unmarried woman. She described the RCIA group sessions as "sort of a mousetrap." When I asked her, "What does that mean?" she replied:

> Well, they all were sitting around like the cat was in the middle of the room; you know, they were not very active. We were all just sitting around like. I mean, none of us really had anything to say, I mean really. Except that we wanted to be Catholics, you know. No one was going to say anything wrong or out of the way. It's a pretty sticky situation; it really is. And you're trying to figure out what they are going to spring on you next that you are not going to know anything about. And it wasn't what I thought it was going to be like at all. I thought it was going to be like—sort of like a catechism class, you know, where you send kids to go to grade school. You send them on Saturday or something, where they learn. And it wasn't; it was sort of like a—Well, they would read a piece of paper and then you would go around the circle. Well, what's your opinion about it?

The hesitancy that Betty mentioned was also cited by Helen. She urged those attending RCIA classes not to be hesitant in asking questions. She said that some people were hesitant because "they're kind of afraid, because to them it's very, very different."

Finally, Lenny, perhaps reflecting his own Jewish training, was struck by the ignorance of the Catholics who were on the RCIA team and of those preparing for confirmation:

And what amazed me, most of these people—I'd say all of these people—were born Catholics and the outstanding ignorance they had of the Bible. I just was amazed; I just—I'd sit there and after I'd have very little input because if I did have any input, I was afraid I would've insulted them or something like that. Because I was really, really amazed at—And particularly the Old Testament, they knew nothing about it; I mean, it was so—it was amazing. I just sat there and wondered where—where—Sure, these were— These were all older people; these were people in their fifties— weren't they?—most of them. What little knowledge they had of the roots of the Catholic faith....

The Breaking Down of Social Barriers

An indication of the impact of the social cohesion on the individuals in this study is exemplified in the descriptions of the breaking down of their own personal barriers, or the often-cited story of the most quiet or reserved member of the group finally breaking down. When asked how her group got along together, Edna stated, "The timidest person, the person that was shyest, eventually ended up being able to say more and more." To her, this was an indication that the group got along "very well." Dave vividly described this occurrence when I asked him, "How did your class get along as a group?"

> Very, very well. I guess probably the greatest experience we had there was when the one that was so uptight broke out into tears and just let it all go. Boy, did we share with her! And, incidentally, our first year down here, we had one of those the same way. Took longer, but when they do that, you know that you're doing it right; you've reached this loving soul and they're finally letting loose and they're reachin' out and say, "Okay, I buy and I accept this. Come on! Help me some more. How do I—How do I continue?" And it's sorta like reachin' up and havin' you help pull up that hill, cuz somebody helped me pull up the hill.

Like many RCIA veterans, Dave, the year after his acceptance into the church, became an active RCIA team member. In his experience as a team member Dave described seeing the more timid members of the class "open like a flower." Reflecting upon the experience of his own group, Dave addressed his approach to the quiet members of the class:

> You'll have somewhere along the line that they'll—everyone will say something, but they just won't open up and you know what's going on, but you encourage that: "Say what you feel like." If they cut off and you see that hesitation, make it easy on 'em. Say, "Okay, Mary, how about you?" They're off the hook. But you got weeks and weeks and weeks—You got all the time in the world.

Deb described the change in younger couples in her group in similar terms: "It was just one of those things they had to do in the beginning. They were being dragged there, and then that changed. It was marvelous to see the change and the growth in those youngsters." Finally, Willard's experience testifies to the breaking down of personal and social barriers:

> Like in our particular classroom, some of 'em kinda were hesitant because they tended to have a rough time through their life—they just weren't open about it, y'know, which is their prerogative; I mean, hey—I think it's very nice. And at that time some of 'em were kinda taken back [sic] with it initially, because they still— y'know, they felt—Well, they weren't Catholic, and "Why are you probing into my life?" Y'know, that type of attitude. But then, after they became friendlier, or more convinced that they were going on, then—then they would open up....

RCIA professionals are coached on quiet or reluctant individuals. They are told, "The catechist is the silence breaker. The first challenge is to get the group to 'open up'" (Kemp, 1979:34). And, "For inquirers who are shy, wounded, afraid, or unable to tell a story or ask questions, or who try end-runs with questions about the minutiae of Catholic practice, ministers will be great listeners" (Dunning, 1981a:47). Furthermore, Dunning states that a time will come when the shy inquirer will "stop playing deuces and discard a face-card" (1981a:47). In such circumstances the RCIA team member is encouraged to make sure that the move toward disclosure is given attention.

My field observations confirm both the level and intention of breaking down personal barriers in the RCIA process. The level of intimate personal disclosures was high. From detailing the deviancy of one's daughter, to telling specifically how one's husband was losing weight, participants spoke freely and deeply about personal matters. At one parish staff meeting I attended, the staff evaluated the level of sharing in the inquirer and sponsor groups. They said the inquirers were sharing better than the sponsors. Someone shared the same thing for two weeks in a row. When he was approached by a staff member who mentioned this duplication, he responded, "You are not supposed to remember what I shared last week." Thus the need for the participants to share personal reflections is addressed and followed up by RCIA teams.

In the prayer group a similar story was told of initial reluctance by the members to "open up" followed by personal disclosure. Sister Agnes began the group as a Bible study but began relating the scriptural passages to personal stories. She said, "So I'm sure the biggest blessing for me was beginning to work with adults and being able to share deep, rich feelings that I haven't been able to share. I've often wondered why the prayer group has meant so much to me. And I think that's it...." Yet Sister Agnes did not feel she "manipulated" the group:

Do you think with the prayer group moving from reading the scriptures to the sharing that goes on now, do you think that was a natural development or do you think it is something that you as the leader of the group facilitated, or allowed? What's your assessment of that?

It could be that I facilitated it. Because it meant so much to me. I never thought of that before. But they seemed to want it. They wanted to know about scripture, but they seemed to want more time for the prayer, sharing prayer. I didn't feel that they felt manipulated. It just seemed to happen that way.

At a seminary class on catechesis, I observed the breaking down of personal barriers in discussing conversion. The class of thirty was divided into five subgroups of six individuals each. The individuals in each group were asked to share some story of conversion from their own experience. The interaction in the small group I observed was uneasy. Eye contact was awkwardly made and then avoided as the first person to tell his story had yet to be decided. Once the first person started, the others followed suit in telling their stories. Yet there were still awkward glances between stories.

After the exercise the professor asked, "What did it [sharing conversion stories] feel like?" Some seminarians told of sharing happily and freely, others shared with reluctance and resistance, but all shared. There was a common theme in the description of those who were resistant in sharing. They stated their resistance but then stated the benefit of the sharing. This seminary exercise gave me insight into the breaking down of social and personal barriers in RCIA groups. Through this exercise the seminarians were taught the reality and value in this breaking down. Group pressure is a powerful force which shows itself rather quickly.

There were social as well as personal barriers that were broken down by the process. Fred is the husband of the woman who spoke of the social benefits of the RCIA. His description of his group indicated that the group followed different social rules and interactions when compared to other societal groups. The age barriers of other social groups were not present:

> So we [Fred and his wife] were by far a great deal older than most of the people there, so you'd think that we really didn't have that much in common socially, but we—we mixed very well with them, but I think on the outside we probably wouldn't have, y'know, gone out socially together, but the whole group was very, very friendly, very warm....

Larry's words endorse Fred's perception: "So it was a mixed group. And the thing that amazed me about it was that we all kind of— just kind of a equalizing force there that just sort of dissolved the age differences."[11]

Significant Others

The RCIA directors are cited by the new Catholics as being very influential in their initiation into the Catholic Church.[12] Often the RCIA directors were cited as individuals who "made a difference" in the people becoming Catholic. One woman described her director in glowing terms, saying, "Ruth is not quite human," and "She's the epitome of a saint." The same woman described the success of their weekly RCIA meetings, saying, "She made it happen." Another woman said, about the religious sister who ran the RCIA in his parish, I "fell in love with her immediately; she's a beautiful person, just lovely; I mean, just—she's so marvelous."

Bud owed his becoming Catholic to a number of Catholic priests. The priest who had initiated the process came to Bud the night Bud's son-in-law was dying. After anointing his son-in-law, the priest talked to Bud about becoming Catholic. "And he signed me up." There were many factors leading to Bud's joining the Catholic Church, but he put it simply: "I don't think I would have become a Catholic if it hadn't been for Father Fred to start with."

The high, positive regard for RCIA directors and clergy reflect Berger and Luckmann's contention that reality is socially defined and social definitions are always embodied in concrete individuals and groups of individuals who serve as definers of reality (1967:116).[13] Yet, Gloria noted the distinction between religion and the group leaders when she spoke of the departure from the parish of the RCIA director and a priest. This was "a real blow." Gloria concluded, "And many of us said, 'Well, what is there left for us? Those two wonderful people are gone.' But the religion itself stayed with us. And so then I was able to work that out."

The admiration for the RCIA directors and clergy was not unanimous. Betty said that she and the director "did not hit it off." Speaking about the director's concern about finalizing Betty's annulment procedure, Betty stated, "She was constantly nagging me, like, 'How's it going? How's it going?'" Summarizing the tension in their relationship, she said, "Yeah, it's never been 'palsies.' You know, I could say 'Good Morning' to her on Sunday and I swear she looks the other way."

Limits to the Social Binding of the RCIA Process

Although the social binding is potent, the binding also appears to be limited to the preparation process. In our interviews there was not a notable mention of a continuation of individual or group relationships after the initiation process was completed. Occasional reunions may occur, but the most common post-initiation interaction cited was "running into each other at mass" on the weekends. One man told of his group getting together after initiation, but once the RCIA director and parish priest moved on to other assignments, "our group kinda fell apart."

Another man went through the RCIA with only one other candidate, a woman, in his class. Although he said he got to know her personally, and to know her life story, he said, "I did not try to carry on any further relationship afterward. I didn't really feel any need. There was no bonding per se as far as I was concerned." Liza stated, "I think everyone felt like they would like this to continue, but our lifestyles were so diverse that it just didn't seem possible for it to happen."

Although few RCIA groups continue in formal relationship after initiation is complete, some people have difficulty in adjusting to life after the group. One woman said that even a year after termination, she still occasionally started to get dressed to go to the group on Monday nights, only to realize the group no longer existed. Deb spoke about the post-RCIA adjustment:

> I'm going to start the Bible study classes next week because I do want to get back and give myself more direction. The support is, I think, the thing you…miss, and it was as if you left your family, because you know this group and its support structure and you're learning and constantly being motivated….

The lack of continuation of relationships beyond the RCIA process is due, in part, to the fact that the RCIA classes are composed of individuals who might not otherwise be socially connected. In other words, the RCIA process is the primary, if not the exclusive, reason for social being.

The example of the prayer group highlights the social importance of the RCIA structure. When the religious sister who was leading the prayer group retired, the members of the group planned to get together once a month for lunch and to stay in touch with one another. One year after its termination the prayer group had yet to meet. The members of the group had been meeting almost every week for four years, canceling doctors' appointments, ignoring arthritic joints, and weathering storms. Yet, once the leader left, the group disintegrated. The leadership offered by the RCIA team may provide a function similar to the function that Sister Agnes offered the prayer group: the time, discipline, and purpose for meeting.

The Easter Vigil: An End and a Beginning

Another factor that may contribute to the lack of continuation of RCIA group interaction is the fact that the RCIA has a natural termination point. The Easter vigil is the ceremony where the rites of initiation are celebrated and the preparation process of the RCIA ends. The participant begins her/his life as a baptized Catholic and ends her/his life as a catechumen. The only formalized aspect of the RCIA after the Easter vigil is the brief period of mystagogy.

The Easter vigil is the most solemn Catholic liturgy of the year. The vigil can last as long as four hours. The vigil serves as a culmination of the process, an experience of group cohesion, and a ceremony of termination from the group. When I asked Fred, "How was the Easter vigil for you?" he replied:

> I enjoyed that because that was togetherness of our group, and we enjoyed being together and going through the ceremony and we were glad that all of the others besides ourself [sic] could do that.

The final acceptance of the RCIA members to full membership in the church is indicated in some parishes by the colors the newly baptized wear. They enter the Easter vigil ceremony wearing brown robes and then, upon baptism and full membership, they change to white robes.[14] Dave addressed the impact of this change of clothing:

> We were in trunks, you know, and we had their brown robes and it really made you feel a part of this whole thing. The symbology was so remindful of where you are, and you are not there, and, and it made you want to reach out and long for this. I could see that white robe, y'know, but I can't wear it because I haven't had eucharist. I haven't had the right—and so you want it. And, yeah, that was—that was a great, great, great thing, to take off the brown robe, dripping wet, dry as quickly as you can, but then put this on.

Finally, Liza described the Easter vigil as "absolutely heavenly." She explained:

> Because to me it gave our whole salvation history. Started with Genesis, went right up to naming our names. What an incredible experience! That's what I wanted in the Catholic Church. And I

found it that night in perfection. You know, it was all spread out there, all the saints mentioned, you know. Oh, awesome![15]

From Private to Public Religiosity

The social nature of the RCIA process was not only evident in attracting and retaining the participants, some participants made conscious decisions to publicly express their religiosity. The social nature of the RCIA was a means of publicly expressing previously privately held beliefs. Peg (Dave's wife) spoke about the mutual decision she and her husband had made to join the church:

> You know, even though we both prayed, we both raised the kids, but you know with grace at meals and things like that, we sort of had our little world as far as our own religion is concerned. And we decided it was time to be mutually—became involved religiously; I think that's the best way to put that, you know.

Peg's statement, along with a frequently expressed concern with neighborhood, national, and global issues (e.g., drugs, education, nuclear weapons, the environment), indicates that these older new Catholics were moving away from the individualism of a "Shielaism" type religion, cited by Bellah and his associates, and toward a more communal outlook (Bellah et al., 1985:221). Their effort to reconstruct their social world includes a more communal and global outlook. Such communal concern among older people is often cited in gerontological literature.

Sharing Life Stories and Group Cohesion

The emphasis on biography and life review in the RCIA process certainly adds to group cohesion. One woman suggested life stories help "you to get closer to people." Liza linked the sharing of life stories with group cohesion: "I think we were sharing so many experiences that there was a beautiful bond that developed among us." Additionally, when I asked Liza, "Do you see any connection between sharing of life stories and becoming a Catholic?" she replied: [pause] "I don't know that there was with becoming a Catholic. But with becoming closer as a group it's incredible. It just works miracles in a group. There's no doubt about that. I've seen it in so many places."

Thus the RCIA may not be simply a plausibility structure for the personal reconstruction of biographies (as detailed in chapter 2); the reconstruction of biographies in small group settings may add to the plausibility of the RCIA process. In this way plausibility is a dynamic, interactive, and two-way reality.

Catholic Beliefs and Membership

The question that the new Catholics consistently found most difficult to answer was, "What Catholic beliefs are appealing to you?" The reasons for this difficulty are related to the sense of belonging. First, the new Catholic was embracing a way of life. Singling out one belief, or a few beliefs, was difficult because the individual "bought the whole package." As Dave said, "You're asking me to break down my religion." Second, the individual joined the church for reasons other than beliefs. Doctrines of the church were utterly secondary for these individuals.[16] Third, the individual was not well-versed in Roman Catholicism. The RCIA does not focus on doctrinal beliefs. Thus the people in this category would feel inadequate to address the question. The social attraction and focus of the RCIA process and Roman Catholicism were more important than Catholic beliefs.

The experience of these new Catholics regarding church teachings or personal beliefs is not unique. Seegar and Kunz found similar difficulty in answering questions among new Mormon converts about their awareness of Mormon beliefs (1972:183). Hoge found that, of those who left the church, in his study, only fourteen percent of those aged twenty-three and over cited specific beliefs as reasons for leaving (cited in Throop, 1986:32). Finally, Greeley has suggested that since Vatican II "the communal Catholic" has emerged. This type of Catholic sees him/herself as a part of the Catholic community and tradition, but not limited by the institutional church (Hoge, 1981:25). The secondary nature of beliefs and teachings for the communal Catholic is reflected in older new Catholics as well.[17]

Social Cohesion and the Prayer Group

In the prayer group many of the same issues of social cohesion, personal identity, and sense of belonging were evident. The prayer group itself was an identifiable body for the members: "our little prayer group," as it was referred to. Membership in the group was closed. On a number of occasions individuals expressed interest in joining the group. Largely through Sister Agnes's advocacy, new members were not invited. Agnes felt the group dynamics would be negatively affected by new members.

An indication of the importance of the group in the lives of its members is evident in the fact that all members of the group have sought admission to the same Catholic nursing home. As Ellen stated, "And it is nice to die with people of your own religion around you," and "To know the church is right under the roof, that's the thing." Ellen suggested that the prayer group itself was responsible for a renewed sense of well-being in her life. She told Sister Agnes, referring to the group, "You have put a whole new person in me!"

Yet there were mixed reactions to the social nature of the Catholic Church today. Joan said that growing up she used to admire the pastors of her Protestant friends who greeted the members of the congregation after the services. She likes the fact that Catholic priests do that now, but,

> I like the closeness, I like that we are able to get together, but sometimes I wonder, Is it all so sincere for some people, or is it a big show? I find it hard to be hugging everyone and saying, "I love you." Because love is more than just touching a person. It is what you feel inside for them. And does everybody really feel that way?

Yet, later in our interview, Karen said that what keeps her going everyday is "getting up in the morning and getting clothes on and coming to mass. And seeing the people that you see there every day, and getting to know them, and to notice when they are missing." Karen then told how she formed a friendship with a woman when she noticed she was not at mass and called to see if she was all right.

Finally, when Joan was told her son had cancer, she literally could not wait for the prayer group to meet. After being restless all weekend, she began the Monday morning meeting by telling the group about her son's diagnosis. She said she had gone to bed early on Sunday night just so the time for the prayer group would come more quickly for her.

The prayer group, then, was a highly significant socially cohesive force in the lives of its participants. Similar to the RCIA participants, the prayer group members found in their meetings a place and environment to share life stories and current crises. Yet, similar to many RCIA groups, the prayer group ceased existing once the leader had departed.

Sense of Belonging Summary

Group cohesion in the RCIA process is strong. As these individuals attempted to make sense of their personal and religious lives, they were attracted to Catholicism. They saw individuals whose happiness indicated they had made sense of their lives. The specific nature of the group resulted, in many cases, in the elimination of common social and age-related barriers to interaction. The cohesion of the groups served to facilitate the initiation process and to provide a social context for the individual's attempt to order his/her life. The RCIA process is a plausibility structure of the first order; that is, it provides a community of people committed to Catholic initiation, interaction with others in the process on a regular and predictable basis, and investment by the participants in the process and in the group.

An apt summary of the influence, the desire for, and attainment of, a sense of belonging comes from Jim, Larry, and Willard. Each tells a story of a growing sense of commitment which led to a change in membership status.

> [Jim]: When I first started goin' to church with Carol [wife] and the kids, I felt like an outsider—I did; felt like I was eavesdropping in. I looked around and I didn't want any of my friends to see me, y'know, that sort of thing, and it got easier and easier and easier, and suddenly I found I wanted to be a part of it, but I couldn't. And now I feel like I'm a full part of it.

Larry echoed Jim's refrain:

> You know, I feel—I feel more accepted, like when I come up to take communion; I feel more a part, not an outsider anymore. Although I was an outsider only in a technical sense, but it has made me feel much closer to my religion and to faith.

Finally, when I asked Willard the reason why he joined the church when he did, he replied, "I felt the Catholic Church really had something to offer me. I was accepted and loved."

Thus one of the answers to the question, "Why do older people become Catholic?" is because they find in the RCIA a place to belong and a structure to support their sense of belonging.

CONCLUSION

Simply looking at the story of one woman demonstrates the variety of motivating factors that are at work in lives of the people I interviewed. Liza was cited in this chapter and in chapter 3 as exemplifying the following traits: longing for a sense of belonging, responding to the challenges of growing older, acting as a seeker, reacting to trauma, and dealing with early childhood memories. Each of these motivating factors finds some resolution in the Catholic community. Berger and Luckmann state, "It is only within the religious community, the *ecclesia,* that the conversion can be effectively maintained as plausible" (1967:158). For Liza, and for many other older new Catholics, the Catholic community represents a source, as well as a maintaining force, for religious commitment and change.

Some people come to the RCIA without any clear notion as to why they are there. They are similar to Barker's characterization of potential Moonies who were searching for something but they did not know quite what it was (1984). Edna implied the lack of clarity and the imposition of reason by the process in saying, "If you want to know why you want to be a Catholic, it (the RCIA process) will tell you. It will help you find out why you really want to be one."

Some individuals come to Roman Catholicism with a clear need and desire to make sense of their world, whether that world be their family life, their faith life, their social life, their life as children, or a combination of factors. Others come, not sure of the questions or the answers, but certain that "something" is needed to make sense of their lives.

Despite the strong social forces in the RCIA, Paula's experience speaks to the powerful individual forces involved in becoming Catholic. At a time when the RCIA was largely an imaginative creation in bishops' minds, Paula became Catholic. Yet her story parallels those of current-day new Catholics with remarkable consistency. In being Catholic she has become a new person. She was a seeker who read all she could about Roman Catholicism. She survived an anti-Catholic home environment in her early childhood, which seems only to add to her self-professed "love" for the church. She was greatly influenced by the example of a Catholic friend at age seventeen. Despite the fact that "most of my good friends of years' standing are anti-religious, and that bothers and hurts me," she found security and identity in the Catholic Church and in her role as a Catholic. She disagreed with some basic teachings of the church and felt the church "has not been fair to women at all." Through the trials and crises of her life, which she said had been many, she learned to "cling to Christ" and "cling to the church."

One could argue that Paula's story is more reflective of her past two decades as a Catholic than it is of her initiation into the church. Yet she entered the church under an entirely different social structure and, twenty-five years after the fact, she shows remarkable similarities with the older new Catholics of the 1990s. To me, the similarities speak to the consistency of autonomous individual actions and the way those joining the church have used various social structures to reach the same personal ends. The similarities also speak to me of the fact that despite all that is new in the RCIA, the power of the social structure of the Catholic Church to inform and mold individuals remains relatively consistent.

Notes

1. Interfaith marriage is relatively common and has gained greater acceptance and approval in the Catholic Church since the Second Vatican Council. For the calendar year 1993, the Archdiocese of Los Angeles reported that out of 13,377 Catholic marriages, 2,005 were interfaith marriages. The Diocese of Fresno reported that of its 2,279 Catholic marriages in 1993, 461 were interfaith marriages (*The Official Catholic Directory: Anno Domini 1994:* 527, 360).

2. The frequency of later-life religious switching in the direction of one's longtime spouse in this study challenges the notion that shifts in membership occur soon after marriage in interfaith couples. (See, for example, Babchuk, Crockett and Ballweg, 1967:552.)

3. Berger and Luckmann suggest that "predecessors" enter the reality of everyday life, "sometimes in a very decisive way" (1967:34). Many people I interviewed addressed their perceptions of how deceased members of their family would react to their becoming Catholic.

4. O'Rourke has criticized the RCIA process for not addressing the

social and family context of the newcomer. Calling the RCIA "a socialization process," O'Rourke warns of an individualistic approach: "A socialization process that undermines already extant and valid social structures, like a marriage, is a process that is proper to a cult, not the Church" (1987: 28).

5. The appeal of having an identity as a convert may relate to the convert role. Society robs elderly people of many of their roles. Becoming a Catholic convert is one way to embrace a new role. Parallels may also be drawn with the religious conversion in adolescents facing identity issues.

6. Maureen's statement indicates she is a "passive convert." Maureen's perspective was shared by another RCIA participant who indicated, "And I was just drawn; I felt that I was really drawn as if I were not making this decision myself."

7. Maureen's description suggests that her role as an inquirer and convert may have been reified. Berger and Luckmann suggest that the paradigmatic formula for the reification of a role is, "I have no choice in the matter, I have to act this way because of my position" (1967:91). This formula is reflected in Maureen's words, "Being a Catholic wasn't a decision I ever had to make."

8. Liza also addressed the benefits of a step-by-step process. During the inquiry stage she found the material redundant and boring. "But after I made the decision to move into the candidate level, I found it much more interesting."

9. Maureen's words reflect Berger and Luckmann's claim that "the institutional order, like the order of individual biography, is continually threatened by the presence of realities that are meaningless in *its* terms" (1976:103). The woman who complained to Maureen did so in terms that were meaningless to Maureen and to the group.

10. The social effects of the emphases of the group activities are not lost on the participants. Clara said that by sharing life stories "you feel more a part of the group; you're not just like a little stranger on the outside."

11. The feelings expressed by Fred and Larry were not endorsed by all the new Catholics. Betty indicated age barriers still existed in her RCIA group:

> I mean, I was lucky, I guess, because there were four or five older people, I mean, my age. Well, even older. And we were young kids, but like I said, I didn't try to sit with the young kids because I don't think that's too cool. You know. They don't want you and I don't want to hear them either. So naturally I gravitated to the older people.

12. In Berger and Luckmann's terms the RCIA directors are often the significant others who mediate the plausibility structure (1967:157).

13. As Berger and Luckmann state:

> What remains sociologically essential is the recognition that all symbolic universes and all legitimations are human products; their existence has its base in the lives of concrete individuals, and has no empirical status apart from these lives (1967:128).

14. The color of robes is just one example of the many overt ways the RCIA process emphasizes that even though the participants are part of the Order of Catechumens, they are not yet full members of the church. The emphasis on new members as solely "inquirers" is another example.

15. The Easter vigil also incorporates symbolism that supports biographical reconstruction. At the vigil, "those who enter fully into the Christian family at this time enter into the death and resurrection of Christ. They die to the old person and rise to the newness of life in Christ" (Anderson, 1986:41).

16. As indicated in the difficulty in naming appealing beliefs, many people joined the church without full knowledge or acceptance of some basic teachings of the church. Nine of the twenty-eight individuals mentioned either birth control or abortion when asked what church teachings they disagreed with or had trouble with. One woman stated:

> And I would have liked to have known a little bit more about the precepts of the Church. What they do is they give you all the sacraments. But when I finished the program, I found I had to find a place that really tells me what the religion is about. And I haven't yet had the time to find something like that.

17. In the prayer group as well doctrinal issues were not primary. Joan, when asked if there is anything she would like to see added or changed in the group, replied, "Well, I really don't think so, unless there would be more Bible reading. Because a lot of it is just talk."

5
Conclusion

MEANING AND BELONGING

Why do older people become Roman Catholic? The stories we have heard from new Catholics suggest that older people become Catholic because they find in Roman Catholicism a source of meaning and/or a source of belonging.

Biographical reconstruction, life review, the other motivating factors for becoming Catholic in later life, and the perspective of Berger and Luckmann, all capture the dual themes of meaning and belonging. Through the life review and biographical reconstruction, individuals assign meaning to their lives, and meaning to life in general. The reality of growing older, the seeker mentality evident in the stories told, the grappling with early childhood memories, and the challenges of crises and transitions in life, all pose questions of meaning. Familial influence and the social aspects of the RCIA are summarized in the notion of belonging. Berger and Luckmann's perspective underlines the importance of finding meaning in personal and social life, and the crucial influence of belonging with significant others and referent groups.

Table 1 gives an overview of the answer to the question "Why do older people become Roman Catholic?" that has emerged from the stories of religious change and commitment in later life.

TABLE 1: WHY DO OLDER PEOPLE BECOME ROMAN CATHOLIC? AN OVERVIEW

Key Passage	Primary Motivating Factor	Primary General Concept
"I look back and think, How many years have I lost? I don't want to lose any more years. I want to start living, I mean **right now**, correctly."	Biographical Reconstruction	Search for Meaning
"As you get older you think, Maybe I better get things squared away before it is too late."	Age	Search for Meaning
"I saw that the Catholics had the answers that I have been longing for but could not find in other religions."	Seeker Mentality	Search for Meaning
"My husband and I, and the trauma that we went through, is part of the reason I guess why I finally ended up in the Catholic Church."	Crisis and Transition in Life	Search for Meaning
"And I wanted to be a part of the church and my family wouldn't let me. And I think in the back of my mind—I thought, Well, someday if I can I—you know, I am going to go on and do it. It took me sixty–one years to do it, but I finally made it."	Early Childhood Memories	Search for Meaning
"I think the most important thing, the satisfying thing is I made my wife really, really happy. I mean, she never pushed or anything like that. I am happy for her because finally it sunk into my thick head."	Familial Influence	Desire to Belong
"I went to a meeting, and I was literally hooked. I didn't know whether to become a Catholic, but I didn't want to leave that [RCIA] group."	Sense of Belonging	Desire to Belong

Meaning

As we age we cannot avoid questions of meaning. Aging challenges us to ask questions, such as, "What is the meaning of life?" and "What has been the meaning of *my* life?" Inasmuch as aging inevitably involves confronting meaning, aging is a spiritual experience. Inasmuch as later life often challenges individuals to consider meaninglessness, later life is a time of spiritual crisis. Aging and spirituality both have meaning at the core (Blazer, 1992).

The stories the older new Catholics have told speak to the meaning they have found in the RCIA and in Roman Catholicism. Through Roman Catholicism they have been able to put their personal biographies in the context of a larger story of a community of faith. The challenges to their lifelong roles that retirement, declining health, the independence of their children, and the inevitability of death have posed have been combatted by accepting the meaning structure of being a convert. They have sought answers to new questions posed by life crises and by seeker mentalities. They have found those answers in Roman Catholicism. By looking as far back as their early childhood, they have dubbed their own lives, and their own stories, as being meaningful and purposeful.

Roman Catholicism offers a schema of meaning for the challenges to meaning that growing old often poses. The storytelling and personal biographical emphases of the RCIA allow the participants to explore meaning in a socially acceptable environment. The American Association of Retired Persons has built an elaborate national volunteer program of reminiscence. The title of the program is, "Reminiscence: Finding Meaning in Memories." In many ways the same title could be applied to the storytelling components of the RCIA, which help people find meaning in memories, and meaning in Roman Catholicism. This meaning is often discovered in and through personal narratives.

Belonging

Roman Catholicism also offers a source of belonging. The desire to move from being an outsider to being an insider, and the desire to move from being a participant to being a member, were constantly mentioned by the older new Catholics. For some individuals meaning is found in belonging. After their baptisms they remain involved in the RCIA as activists and team members. They feel like better people, more enhanced and more enriched, precisely because they belong. The RCIA period is a time of intensive personal interaction. The social cohesion that results from the group emphases of the RCIA is very powerful. Even though many participants do not continue personal relationships on an intensive level with other new Catholics after baptism, the casual meetings with other new Catholics at church services seem to rekindle many of the positive social feelings experienced during the process.

The sense of belonging was evident particularly in the attraction people felt to the social aspects of the RCIA and the desire people expressed to unify their family in one religion. In many cases, being the only non-Catholic in the family, this desire translates into people wanting to fully belong to their own family.

LESSONS FROM THE STORIES OF OLDER NEW CATHOLICS

The lessons the older persons have told in the narratives of becoming Catholic extend beyond the importance of meaning and belonging in later life. Their stories speak to various levels of their own experience and various levels of past research on religious conversion and membership switching.

Religion is an intensely personal and an intensely social phenomenon. Through listening to the personal and social reflections of older new Catholics, we have heard of the intensely personal and intensely social dynamics involved in the decision to join a religion. Here are some of the facts that the narratives of older new Catholics reveal:

- Old age is not a time of religious stagnation. Rather, for many of these people, old age is a time of radical religious change.
- The older new Catholics in this study, despite sharing many common features (for example, Caucasian residents of Southern California who became Catholic in later life), are a diverse and dynamic group. The diversity of their lives is evident especially in the stories they told of how they became Catholic.
- Decisions to join the Catholic Church are based far more on personal and family relationships than on doctrinal issues or matters of religious belief.

- The attractions of the Roman Catholic Church to the people I interviewed are as diverse and varied as their life experiences.
- The RCIA is a very effective instrument in accomplishing the goal of introducing potential new members "to a community of 'fellow travelers'" (Dunning, 1981b:178). According to these new Catholics, the RCIA is not effective in conveying Catholic beliefs or doctrines.
- The social cohesion of RCIA groups is a powerful and explicitly intended force. As one RCIA advocate states, "Let us respect the need for all sorts of gestures of human friendship and small talk before people trust each other enough to share their lives" (Dunning, 1981b:181).
- Biographical reconstruction is present in dramatic terms in the stories of some of the new Catholics. For many, but not all people, biographical reconstruction was found to be a motivating factor and/or an indicator of the change involved in becoming Catholic in later life.
- There is an autobiographical component built into the RCIA process which serves as a plausibility structure for the social reconstruction of biographies. By telling stories, the inquirers come to perceive the church as "we" and not as "they" (Dunning, 1981b:183). They find meaning and belonging in their lives.
- For both the lifelong Catholics and the new Catholics the concept "religious conversion" was not decisive; rather "becoming Catholic" or "being Catholic" was the decisive concept.
- Some of the stories contradict commonly held notions about religious change. For example, changes of religious affiliation are supposed to occur in the period soon after marriage until the birth of the first child. Yet many older new Catholics waited decades until "the time was right" to become Catholic.

God and Religion in the Stories of Becoming Catholic

Contrary to past research, the older new Catholics have told us that joining a religion does not necessarily require self-change, or changing a worldview (Kilbourne and Richardson, 1989:15). Remarkable, given the RCIA's strong emphasis on religious conversion, is the lack of willingness of older new Catholics to claim personal religious conversions. Despite the fact that the RCIA *requires* religious conversion, nearly half of the people I interviewed indicated they did not have a religious conversion. They freely called themselves "converts" but denied a religious conversion.[1]

Some people spoke of their decision to join the Catholic Church in vivid words and images that related directly to their relationship with God or their religious faith (for example, Dave and Reverend Jones). Others told the story of their becoming Catholic in words and images that largely excluded references to God or religion (for example, Betty and John). When reviewing the interviews as a whole, one is left with the sense that a special or unique *religious* expression of becoming Catholic is largely absent from the narratives. Sociologically, this is perhaps the most surprising finding, of many surprising findings. I expected religious motivations and expressions to be more common among older people who became Catholic. I expected the search for meaning and belonging in later life to be told in religious terms. I expected biographical reconstruction to take a specifically religious form in later life.

The fact that God and religion are not emphasized in the narratives can be attributed to a number of factors: First, some people simply did not become Catholic for religious or God–related reasons. For some people, the unity of their family, the desire to belong, and the coping mechanism that the Catholic Church offered were reasons enough to become Catholic. The prayer group members, on the other hand, initially signed up for a Bible study, which evolved into a prayer group. Their frame of reference from the start was explicitly God-and religion-related.

Second, some people lacked the experience, socialization, and/or vocabulary to talk religiously. At one RCIA meeting I was stunned at the questions one young woman asked me, not knowing I was a priest, about God and the views of Roman Catholicism. Her questions were of the nature: Who is God? How was the world created? Who is this Jesus we are talking about? Many people come to the RCIA, and many people complete the RCIA process, without a religious frame of reference. The prayer group, on the other hand, was born and bred in the religious language and images of the Catholic Church. Religious and God-related images permeate the stories of the prayer group members.

Third, the approach I took as an interviewer may have influenced people's frame of reference. I emphasized my researcher role and deemphasized my priest role. The questions I asked were largely separated from God and religion. One possible avenue for future research would be to conduct a similar study, but in an explicitly religious framework. As a comparison study, I would present myself as a priest and ask such religiously oriented questions as, "Who is God for you?" and "Was your decision to become Catholic related to your personal relationship with Jesus Christ?" The influence of the researcher-versus-priest approach seems even more possible given the fact that, in the experience and perception of the prayer group members, I was much more a priest and much less a researcher. Once again, religious images were far more prevalent in the prayer group meetings and stories when compared to the RCIA meetings and stories.

The Complexity of Life and the Lack of Complexity of Theory

A theoretical approach that describes or explains conversion or religious joining only in terms of sociocultural factors, environmental realities, and social forces neglects the full reality in which an individual lives (Richardson, 1985:172). The separation of personal and social factors, and the separation of meaning and belonging, are possible only in theory. The stories of older new Catholics, their language, experiences, and social settings, have moved us beyond a theory of religious conversion to the reality of social and religious change in the lives of older Americans.

By focusing on the narratives of individuals, we have moved beyond a stale approach to denominational switching. Instead we have identified factors in denominational switching that have largely been ignored in past research: conscious, rational decisions by individuals, specific congregations and their appeal, influences of priests and other significant others, developmental issues of aging, and the like. In short, we have identified aspects of membership switching that are distinct from religious conversion and that are not easily identifiable by survey research.

In the past, theories of religious conversion and membership switching have discussed clear, precise, and neat categories such as religious conversion, membership, and religious experience. Models have presented the normative way individuals convert and come to a religion. The narratives in this study suggest people simply do not live in sociological categories. Individuals do not fall into precise typologies.

The stories told by older people in answering why they became

Roman Catholic are marked by their complexity. Why are their stories complex? Two reasons emerge from their stories: First, by becoming Catholic these individuals are attempting to make sense of their worlds (that is, to find meaning). And their worlds are complex. Their worlds consist of differing modes of time, differing familial and social relationships, differing roles and expectations, and differing environments. They have lived long and so they have much to integrate. To try to integrate the varying personal and social stimuli into one meaningful system is a complex task.[2]

Second, these individuals are joining a mainline religion. The narrow recruiting focus of new religious movements, of cults and of sects, is not present in Roman Catholicism. The individual has a broad religious framework in which to integrate broad personal and social concerns. One reason that past research has not upheld the complexity of joining a religion may be that the reasons for, and means of, joining a cult or sect are less complex than the reasons for, and means of, joining a mainline religion. As Mark Suchman has suggested, "...radical religious reorientations on the fringe are conceptually distinct from membership shifts in the mainstream" (Suchman, 1992:S16). Future research would help clarify the similarities and differences in joining cults and mainline religions. The questions, approaches, and analysis of this study are well-suited for comparison with similar questions, approaches, and analysis of conversion and/or membership switching to sects or cults.

The Lessons of Personal Narrative and Life Stories

Each person's story is unique and rich. Sociology's challenge is to once again embrace life stories and personal narratives. By embracing life stories and personal narratives, sociologists will include the remembered past as a sociological fact in the present. Sociologists who dismiss memories as "subjective," and thus not relating to "real" events, are neglecting the power, purpose, and place of memories in personal biographies and in social realities.[3]

Without a personal narrative approach, with particular focus on the telling of one's story, the early childhood influences that were so prominent in the stories of becoming Catholic may not have been discovered. Perhaps the surprise of the early childhood findings lies, not in the prominence of such experience, but in the absence of consideration of the social impact of early childhood experiences in other religious conversion literature.

Sociological Inertia

Religious conversion and membership switching have been exemplary topics for a narrative approach to sociology. As David O'Rourke states, "The experience of conversion highlights our human elements with uncommon intensity. Few of life's experiences bring into such sharp focus the personal history, the current issues and the agenda that make us who we are" (1987:1).

For sociological creativity and imagination to flourish, the researcher and theorist must confront the historical and institutional inertia of sociology. In general, sociologists deemphasize the individual level. Partly because of the newness of the field, and partly because of the desire to be "socially scientific," sociologists are very cautious about becoming too close to psychology in their approach. The result is approaches to social reality that can be distant from individual experience and everyday life. Instead of speaking about complementary approaches we speak of micro versus macro, qualitative versus quantitative, and psychology versus sociology. The history of the sociology of religious conversion is one of paradigm conflict (Richardson, 1985).[4] The paradigm conflict within the sociology of conversion reflects and reproduces paradigm conflict within sociology in general.[5]

As I have emphasized, there is a dialectical relationship between the teller and the social context in which one tells his/her story. Sociology of conversion literature has been too complacent in accepting characterizations such as "active" or "passive" convert. Is the older new Catholic more the passive product of social forces *or* an active agent in social and personal change? The stories of the older people in this book tell us that the group, and individuals in the group, are both passive and active. They are both formed by social forces and active agents in social and personal change. Individuals and groups simply do not fall neatly into a passivist or activist category. The narratives of these individuals suggest that the opposition of activist and passivist paradigms is a false dichotomy.

Through an approach that recognizes and analyzes the social and personal dialectic, we have moved beyond the one-sided sociological perspective of individual behavior being a consequence of social organization, and of personality being an outcome of social learning (Neugarten and Datan, 1973:55). Rather, while recognizing the influence social structures can have, especially on passive individuals, we have reintroduced the individual as an active social actor.

Theoretical Perspectives on Religious Conversion

At the outset of this project, one of my goals was to utilize the stories of older new Catholics to build a theory of religious conversion and membership switching in later life that speaks to their experience. Yet their narratives and experiences have taught me there is not a *single* theory of religious conversion in later life. If, as Duggan suggests, there are "nearly as many typologies suggested as there are researchers" (1984b:122), then one might conclude typologies are serving more the interests of the researcher than they are serving the experience of the converts. Just as no single explanation could be cited to account for conversion in one individual so, too, no single theory can account for conversion in a group of older new Catholics.

For the sociology of religion, one lesson of this research is that we can present data that are rich in the religious language and images of people without being "religious sociologists." This study has contributed to what Taylor calls the "sociology of religious talk" (Taylor, 1976:19). Included in the sociology of religious talk is concern with, not so much what people say about religion, but how people talk religiously. We have moved beyond sociological speculation relating to observed religious behavior to sociological presentation of religious experience narratives. The result is a reorientation of theoretical perspective for the sociology of religion (Taylor, 1976:17).

In addition to asking "Who are the older converts?" we have asked, "How are older people converting?" In short, we have tapped the level of meaning that past survey research has been unable or unwilling to tap.[6] In the end, we have found meaning to be a key issue in the lives of older new Catholics. Additionally, labeling a sequence of stages, as many theories of conversion do, does not necessarily specify the causal relationships or motivating factors of conversion (Snow and Machalek, 1984:184). Sociologists of religion have devoted too much effort to identifying the causes of conversion and too little effort to listening to the answers to the question, "Why did you convert?"

To the sociology of age and the life course, this book, and the stories that have been told, offer a multidimensional vision of religiosity in later life. By letting people talk religiously, we have presented what religiosity means to aging individuals. We have moved beyond a behavioral gerontological approach which focuses on "religious" activities to consider the older person as an acting agent. Similar to the sociology of religious conversion, the sociology of aging needs to incorporate the fact that religiosity is not measured solely by the level of public religious activity and private religious devotions. Religiosity in later life is also indicated in the way aging people talk religiously. The religious nature of their decision making and motivation is revealed in the language and images they use. As mentioned above, a future comparative study with a more explicitly religious approach could contribute even further to the sociology of religious talk.

One of the reasons why the experiences of those who join churches in *later life* have been all but forgotten by sociologists may be that previous models, as far back as the seminal work of William James, have dictated that adolescence and young adulthood are the normative times for conversion. This study has allowed the older voices to be heard. The words and experiences of these older new Catholics speak to research and theories on religiosity and aging. Instead of speculating on the effects of age on religious activity, we directly asked the people about their experiences. Despite the contrary trends noted in research (Levin, 1988), the stories we have heard suggest that old age can be a time of increased religious activity as well as increased religiosity. Yet for some people, increased religious activity was not accompanied by increased religiosity. By listening to their experiences, we are challenged to greater precision in theory and research on religiosity and aging.

Lessons for Past Theories of, and Approaches to, Religious Conversion

Many past theories of, and approaches to, religious conversion would have discounted the value of the stories of older new Catholics. Their stories would be seen as unique cases. Yet by listening to the stories of new members of the Catholic Church, we have brought into the sociology of conversion the accounts of mainline members and older members. If past theories of conversion do not speak to the experience of older Roman Catholics, then one needs to look not only at the uniqueness of the experience of older converts to a mainline religion but also at how this uniqueness challenges accepted theories.

By listening to the personal narrative accounts of older new Catholics, we have been led to precision in our conceptualization of religious conversion and membership switching. Simply stated, an individual may have remarkable changes in church-related activity and not claim to have had a religious conversion. Such a combination has not been examined in past research. Some individuals joined the Catholic Church without even a hint of religious conversion in their lives. We have examined aspects and influences on their decision to join the Catholic Church without the presumption that because they joined the Catholic Church they have had a religious conversion. Without this presumption, we have been free to examine influences that may have been ruled out in a theoretical approach that assumes religious conversion. For example, the social attraction of the group and family socialization are influences and aspects that deserve at least as much attention as personal religious conversion.

On the other hand, social networks should not be dismissed as solely influencing membership and not influencing religious conversion. Snow and Machalek state, "Social networks are very important in explaining how people are recruited into new religious movements and organizations" (1984:182). The stories of older new Catholics suggest that social networks influence religious conversion as well as religious joining.

To borrow an analogy stated by one participant in this study, I do not think cozy little theoretical boxes of religious conversion research can speak directly to the diverse experience of religious and membership change. While recognizing the commonalities, themes, and categories which are present in the stories of becoming Catholic in later life, we have also seen that particular aspects and segments of individual stories are equally fruitful for analysis. While looking at particular aspects of the conversion process, one can also identify commonalities in the aspects.

In brief, sociology of conversion literature as a body presented theoretical notions, definitions, and categories which simply did not account for experiences of older new Catholics. What is religious conversion? Up until now the answer may have been, "It depends on which theorist you ask." In this study the answer is, "It depends on which new Catholic you ask." The shift in focus is fundamental and foundational. Sociological research and theory in religious conversion will be better served in the twenty-first century if we devote our efforts, not first to revealing the theoretical vision of the researcher, but first to revealing the lived experience of conversion and membership switching.

CONCLUSION

Even though the conclusions we have reached are only representative of the people who have participated in this study, still, the lessons we have learned speak to sociologists, gerontologists and RCIA professionals. In many ways this book is a first step in the research of this field, with many implications which can be pursued in other fields of interest.

Rather than treating converts as social products to be explained, we have approached them as individuals with unique stories to tell about the dynamics of social production. Narrative accounts both explain the particular attraction of conversion to a certain religion and reveal the range of circumstances under which people are converting (Heirich, 1977:657). In short, this book is a call to consider the content of conversion as revealed in narratives, as well as the social context that is often revealed in theorists' typologies.

The stories we have told, and the conclusions we have reached, give much empirical support to the theoretical perspectives of Berger and Luckmann. The influence of family members and significant others has been extraordinarily strong in the stories of becoming Catholic. Yet a theory that details only the influence of other people would be inadequate to capture the stories we have been told. Berger and Luckmann write, "It would, therefore, be a mistake to assume that only significant others serve to maintain subjective reality. But significant others occupy a central position in the economy of reality-maintenance" (1967:150). Berger and Luckmann have a grand theoretical vision, but not a grand theory. Their dialectic has resulted in much fruitful individual and structural analysis in this study.

Additionally, Berger and Luckmann's advocacy of the importance of everyday life and the reality of the remembered past has served this study well. Focusing on everyday life has allowed us to examine personal and social reality as it is real for older new Catholics. Berger and Luckmann linked the notions of religious conversion and community in a dynamic relationship. The intimate connection of conversion and community was constantly affirmed and proclaimed in the stories of becoming Catholic in later life. A focus on the remembered past has resulted in a view of social reality that is dynamic in the modes of time.

The stories I was told, and the analysis of the stories, show that Berger and Luckmann have provided more than a good frame for this study. Their relatively speculative theory of twenty-five years ago speaks directly, dramatically, and precisely to the experience of older new Catholics. Even the vivid language that the people used is reflective of Berger and Luckmann's theory (for example, finding "security" and "identity" in the Catholic Church, and trying to "correct" one's life story). Whether they were discussing death, childhood memories, the influence of a spouse, or the images of dead relatives, the new Catholics consistently affirmed, in very specific ways, the theoretical vision of Berger and Luckmann.

Our analysis of religious conversion and membership switching suggests that theoretical reflection, removed from grand causal schemes, is now appropriate in the sociology of conversion. Researchers and theorists ought to devote some of their attention to theoretical insights relating to various aspects of the process of religious change. Some of these aspects have been addressed here: biographical reconstruction, family influence, sense of belonging, seeker mentality, realities of aging, early childhood memories, and transitions in later life. Past typologies of religious conversion have been helpful in identifying key attributes of conversion experiences (Gartrell and Shannon, 1985:32). Yet they have largely isolated some attributes at the expense of others. To try to link the various motivating factors identified in this study together in a grand theory of religious conversion and membership switching in later life would be a disservice to the experience of older new Catholics and to the discipline of sociology. Rather, a task for further research is to explore the various theoretical nuances of each aspect based on the personal narratives of those involved in the process.

What about biographical reconstruction? Biographical reconstruction, like the other six factors we have examined, is certainly an important aspect of both religious conversion and religious joining among the participants in this study. Biographical reconstruction is hard work. Many older new Catholics exuded a sense of accomplishment and confidence in resolving many life issues. Ida's experience comes immediately to mind. Recall that Ida delayed cancer treatments until after her baptism. When I asked her, "Do you have any goals that you would like to accomplish in the years ahead?" with an enormous smile and enthusiasm she proclaimed, "I have accomplished my goal!" Other people demonstrated that the hard work of biographical reconstruction is rarely completed. John's grappling with his son's sudden death, and the emergence of death as an issue in my interview with Dave are two examples that once again come immediately to mind.

Thus biographical reconstruction is only one aspect of the conversion process. Biographical reconstruction takes on various forms, and shows a variety of impacts, in the stories of becoming Catholic. By itself, biographical reconstruction is inadequate to account for conversion. We began with an attempt to examine a monocausal theory of religious conversion in the life stories of older new Catholics; through our narrative sociological approach we have come to a dynamic presentation of multiple aspects of religious conversion and membership switching.

In 1978, James Beckford initiated a theoretical discussion of religious conversion which continues to this day. Beckford's main task was to "account for conversion." After nearly two decades, the time has come to move beyond accounting for conversion through broad theoretical generalizations and to begin reconstructing the way sociologists deal with biographical data. We must continue to ask questions and seek answers based on the stories people tell. Rich, diverse, reality-based theories of religious change in life will be greatly advanced through the faithful telling of conversion stories.

This book has served to bring the convert, his personal narrative and her life story, back into conversion literature. By bringing the personal narrative back in, we have listened to and presented the stories of older individuals who, through joining the Catholic Church, have added a sense of meaning and belonging to their life stories.

As a sociologist my intention has been to bring the art and science of sociology into a dialogue with the stories of religious change and commitment in later life. Throughout this book I have focused on what we have learned sociologically from these stories. Yet, as a priest, I have learned much from these older new Catholics as well. They have both challenged and strengthened my faith. Through them I have a better sense of "the person in the pew." I have heard phenomenal stories of God's activity in people's lives. I have also heard that some people become Catholic for reasons utterly separated from God and religion. As a priest, the lack of an explicitly religious motivation in the stories of becoming Catholic has been the most challenging and disturbing finding. When I presented some of my findings to a seminary class, the students largely felt the findings were "sobering" and represented "reality." In many ways I concur with the assessment of the class members.

Yet, as a priest and as a Christian, I know that God works always and everywhere through human lives and through human stories. Even though some people I interviewed were not able to put into words the reality of God in their stories of becoming Catholic, I trust that God was very much present and active in their lives. I hope that, in time, and with the support of their Catholic and Christian communities, they will be able to name God's presence in their lives. Because of their stories I have made an effort to make my sermons more challenging, and hopefully more compelling. I find myself speaking more and more with the people about the center of our faith as Catholics. Since this study began, I have been more conscious and deliberate about challenging people in our congregation to consider what being a Christian means to them and why they are Catholic Christians.

Although the social aspect of the RCIA was very attractive for many of the older new Catholics, I would caution against emphasizing the social nature of the RCIA at the expense of the spiritual nature. William Sims Bainbridge's review of the sociology of conversion in the *Handbook of Religious Conversion* (1992) captures this caution well:

> As Dean Kelly has shown...it can be fatal to stress the social life of the church to the exclusion of its religious life. Social influence is the medium of transmission of faith, and it can do much to sustain faith. But unless people have a religious yearning, and unless religion offers people something distinctively different from what any social club can give, faith will wither (Bainbridge, 1992:184).

I find the stories older new Catholics tell to be very affirming of the life-story aspects of the RCIA process. Particularly for older adults, the formal sharing of life stories in the RCIA presents an enormous opportunity for human growth and spiritual maturity. I see God's grace very active in the life story focus of the RCIA. The RCIA provides a place for people to age in the Spirit.

Yet, I also take very seriously the concern I have heard over and over again of the feeling of a lack of true knowledge about God and Catholicism at the completion of the RCIA process. RCIA planners would be well advised to capitalize both on the value of storytelling and on the yearning RCIA participants have to come to know and love God in the community of the Catholic Church.

Through sociological analysis I have gained a greater understanding of the RCIA and of "what makes older new Catholics tick." Through listening to the fascinating stories of older new Catholics my sociological, priestly, and human horizons have been expanded immensely. In 1918, when sociology was in its infancy, Max Weber wrote: "Age is not decisive; what is decisive is the trained relentlessness in viewing the realities of life, and the ability to face such realities and to measure up to them inwardly" (1946:126-127). Facing the realities of life and measuring up to them inwardly is precisely what these older new Catholics have done.

Notes

1. As with Beckford's study of Jehovah's Witnesses, the older new Catholics in this study expressed an unconventional view of religious conversion. Yet contrary to those in Beckford's study the older new Catholics did not express a view of religious conversion that was consistent with the teachings of the group (Beckford, 1978:258).

2. One recent work which has recognized the complexity of religious conversion and membership switching is Lewis Rambo's *Understanding Religious Conversion* (1993). Rambo writes:

> Motives, after all, are not simple and single. They may be multiple, complex and often quite malleable. For instance, when a person first comes into contact with a religious movement, his or her motives for conversion may be to achieve prestige, a sense of belonging, or other extrinsic rewards. After a period of interaction, however, the person may change his or her rhetoric of motives, as deep spiritual or religious yearnings and aspirations are triggered. People change over time, and so do their motives. Indeed, change is the essence of conversion. There is certainly no one motive for conversion (p. 140).

3. An example of the combination of objective past and subjective present comes from Reverend Jones' comments about the death of his wife. The objective fact is that his wife died weeks before he sought membership in the church. This fact can be verified by checking death certificates and meeting dates between Reverend Jones and the priest who gave him instruction. The subjective recall of Reverend Jones is that he needed comfort and care when his wife died, and he found it in the church. Whether or not, objectively, at the time, Reverend Jones felt these needs, the perceived feeling of these needs and his perceived response of the church have been influential in his becoming Catholic. I interviewed Reverend Jones one week after his baptism. An interview with him five years from now could help to put the objective past and subjective present into further temporal perspective.

4. William Sims Bainbridge's advocacy of a combined approach when using strain theory and social influence theory is an example of an approach which diminishes paradigm conflict. Unfortunately, strain theory and social influence theory are more often viewed as *competing* theories of religious conversion (Bainbridge, 1992:178–179).

5. The emphasis on complementary paradigms, as opposed to competing paradigms, presented by this research has applications as well in the sociology of aging. For example, J. Brandon Wallace has suggested that the life review is not a natural process of aging, but "a social activity, growing out of and shaped by narrative challenges posed in the course of interaction" (1992: 121). There is no reason why Butler *and* Wallace are not both correct in their analyses. Wallace sees his perspective as in opposition to Butler's perspective. Life review is presented as initiated in social interaction and thus a social, rather than a personal, construction.

6. The questions we have asked, and the level of meaning we have identified, parallel the perspective and approach of Max Weber, particularly as discussed in *The Methodology of the Social Sciences* (1949).

Appendix A
The Confessions of a Priest Researcher

The fact that I am a Roman Catholic priest brought a dimension to this research which I was aware of, sensitive to, and documented throughout the project. This appendix will present the perspectives of the people I interviewed on the fact that I am a priest and my own reflections on being a priest researcher.

The issues I address here are issues for every researcher. Researchers are never apart from the social worlds which they study. Every researcher faces questions of the comfortability of roles and the ways in which she or he interacts with the people being studied.[1]

BACKGROUND

Before beginning the research phase of the project, I weighed the pros and cons of concealing my identity as a priest. The obvious reason to conceal my identity would be that presenting myself as a priest might bias the participants; that is, they might respond to me as they would expect me as a priest to want them to respond. Every person I interviewed had a preconceived image of what a priest is.

On the other hand, concealing my identity as a priest might have resulted in an awkward situation if individuals discovered I was a priest. Since I attended RCIA public meetings, and I was active in public ministry, and since establishing trust and rapport with older new Catholics was important, this appeared to be a substantial risk.

There appeared to be many benefits to presenting myself as a priest: First, I felt that access and entree would be secured more easily, both to the RCIA directors for obtaining the names and addresses of older new Catholics, and in getting myself welcomed into people's homes or apartments. Second, Roman Catholicism emphasizes openness and trust in relationships with priests. Since priests are confessors and pastoral counselors, many people tell priests things they would tell no one else. This also presented a possible confounding issue; that is, people might mistake my role as that of a confessor rather than as a researcher. Yet confession has a unique form, and usually a unique place, in Roman Catholicism.

In the end, I decided not to conceal my identity as a priest. The potential gains in access, entree, and openness seemed to at least balance the possibility of biasing the participants in the research. Additionally, there was a level of personal comfort involved. Quite simply, I did not feel comfortable concealing my identity as a priest when I met face-to-face with individuals to discuss issues relating to Catholicism. Ethically and morally I felt that as a priest, and as a researcher, I should not conceal my identity.

Even though I presented myself as a priest, efforts were made to mitigate possible bias. First, I dressed in casual clothes; I did not wear a priest's black shirt and collar (known as "clerics").

Second, in my initial phone conversations, although I identified myself as "Father Rich Erikson from St. John's Seminary," I added, "Although I am a priest, I am also a researcher in the Sociology Department at the University of Southern California. I am calling you today as a researcher." Additionally, before each interview began, I stated, and then gave each individual a written statement that said in part, "Although I am a priest, I am here today as a researcher. I do not represent the Archdiocese of Los Angeles or the RCIA office. Your answers have no influence on your standing as a Catholic. Your participation in this research is totally voluntary. If at any time you wish to stop the interview you may do so without any penalty." In addition to these written and oral comments, I stated: "I do not think there are any right or wrong answers to these questions. I am only interested in your honest response to the questions, how you really feel about what I will be asking you."

Third, I monitored the reaction of individuals to me during the study. Each individual was asked to discuss the fact that I am a priest. In my field observations I was sensitive to interactions that seemed influenced by my being a priest. On three occasions during field observations I did wear clerics. Twice I was involved in a public liturgy. The other occasion was a training session at the archdiocesan offices.

THE REACTIONS OF OLDER NEW CATHOLICS AND PRAYER GROUP MEMBERS

My assessment is that wearing lay clothes helped mitigate any possible bias that being a priest may have posed. The people I talked with rarely referred to me as "Father." Few people approached me with the degree of distance or mode of respect that I often feel when I function as a priest.

Near the end of each interview I asked each person to comment on the fact that I am a priest. I attempted to present the question in such a way as to suggest that treating me differently was natural and even to be expected. In each interview I presented the same situation. A verbatim quotation from one interview demonstrates the nature of the question and the scenario I presented in each interview:

> Y'know, sometimes the fact that I'm a priest means that people treat me a little bit differently. If I stopped on the way from Camarillo here today to pick up a newspaper dressed as I am, I'd walk in the store, get the newspaper, leave—that would be it; but if I went in with a black shirt and white collar, people would say, "Hello, Father. Isn't it warm today?"...So people do naturally treat me different. I'm wondering if the fact that I'm a priest has influenced our conversation.

After each person answered this question, I would follow up with: "Do you think if there was another researcher here who wasn't a priest, you might have handled the questions differently?" Alternatively I would ask: "If there were another researcher here from USC, do you think you would have handled the interview any differently?"

Not one person stated that my being a priest negatively affected our conversation. Twenty out of twenty-eight participants initially answered "no," my being a priest did not influence the interview. Yet after the probe question was posed, many did offer insights into how my being a priest did positively affect the interview.

Those who answered with an unqualified "no" did so with conviction. Larry said, "I've tried to be just totally honest with you and open and not con you or look better than I should." In response to the probe question he said, "I feel very comfortable with you. And I can be honest with you."

A few people mentioned the fact that priests were human too, or priests were people too. Two people mentioned negative experiences with priests to highlight this fact. Jim told the story of a priest who was flirting with his daughter and three other girls at a dinner he attended:

> That's where he was all day; he never stirred away from 'em. And I commented to my son-in-law: "What the hell's goin' on over there? The only thing he's interested in is those four young girls. Is he a priest? Is he a real priest or is he just in school or what's goin' on?" "No, he's a real priest." Don't you know, he started writing love letters to my daughter and we raised hell with my daughter.

Jim concluded, "They are priests, they are of the cloth, but they have human emotions; they are human beings just like you and me." The fact that Jim would tell me, a priest, this story is indicative of the level of openness and honesty I felt in our interview. Interestingly, he said priests are human beings "just like you and me." This seems to imply that Jim did not perceive me as a priest. When I asked him the follow-up question, he said that he had probably been "more honest than I should."

Jim is not the only individual who did not appear to perceive me as a priest. Two people said they "forgot" I was a priest. Even though one of these interviews took place in my office at the seminary, Maureen said, "I forgot you were a priest." Another woman said, "I keep forgetting it, quite frankly." One woman seemed confused when I asked her the question and said, "When we were talking you didn't tell me right away, I don't think, that you were a priest, or did you?"

A number of people, while denying that being a priest was influential, suggested that the fact I was Catholic was a positive factor. June said, "I would talk better to you because you are Catholic, okay? I probably would because I'd feel you're more understanding, whereas some people might go, 'Oh, that poor old lady, she's crazy.'" Liza said priests are "just fellow Christians," but said she may have approached the interview with me differently than with another USC researcher: "I might have felt that unless he had a religious background that he might not understand as well what I am saying. I have felt that you would understand it better because of your spiritual background."

With some individuals there was a level of disclosure that may have been related to my being a priest. Willard described in detail a vision of Jesus Christ he had while in battle during World War II. Following his description he said, "I never told that to anybody." Ted said, "I feel so close to the Catholic religion and to the priests as a whole...that I throw a little bit more out of my life."

Two women mentioned my youth as an issue. Betty, when I asked her if her values or beliefs had changed over time, said, "Well, of course at your age, what do you know? But things do change. I mean even at thirty your ideas change. And get to be sixty and they change even more." Paula, the prayer group member who became Catholic, indicated my youth was an issue, not my priesthood:

> My feeling is that you are doing the very best you can as a young man, not as a priest, but as a young man. I have some feeling that I was thinking about some of the things that I ought to tell you and then I would say, "He's too young; he won't quite grasp this. He will when he gets to be possibly half my age, but the young do not see things as an older person does." In the first place, you see we are—I'm going downhill rapidly. I am eighty-seven now and I hope I don't live to be over ninety, but I may. And we don't—A lot of things when we are younger we use [inaudible] because you don't want to expose this to other people. At my age we are soon going to be gone, so bring it out. And it would be your youth, not the fact that you are a priest.

A number of people were confused and seemed to be so because of my attire. One man's wife asked if I was a priest before the interview and asked if I was ordained after the interview. Betty, who commented on my age, also commented on my attire:

So I'm wondering if the fact that I am a priest influenced at all what we are talking about tonight?

You'll probably be insulted.

No, go right ahead.

> The way you are [her hand sweeps, indicating my sitting position and clothes, probably noting the black leather-bound notebook prominent in my lap], it's like talking to a sociologist or an engineer or, I mean, Joe Blow, you know.
>
> *Mm-hum.*
>
> No, I'm not scared, I'm not impressed, but you're right. If you had the white collar on [she holds her hand high on her neck] and the black, I'd probably think, Oh, my God!, you know. It does make a difference; I mean it. It makes you nervous in the first place because he is dressed like that; I guess that's it. And it's hard to talk to them like a human being unless you know them.

Once again, notice that Betty describes priests as if I were not a priest. She talks of "him" and "them," not "you." Betty again mentioned her perception of my youth (this time by saying "you're," recognizing that I am a priest): "But I know that you're all just human, you know, everyday twenty-eight-year-old or twenty-five-year-olds or whatever it is." (For the record, at the time of the interview, I was thirty-three years old.)

When I called people to schedule interviews, I gave them the choice of meeting me at their place of residence, at a local parish office, or at the seminary. Four people met me at a local parish office. Two people met me at the seminary. A woman who met me at the seminary commented on the fact I was in "lay clothes" after the interview. I asked her if this surprised her. She said it did not because she met me at the seminary. If I came to her home, she would have expected me to be in priest clothes.

As her comments about my youth may have indicated, the most reluctant individual in this study was Paula. She had had some very difficult life experiences that she was hesitant to talk about. But when I asked her for permission to tape the interview she said, "I trust you implicitly." In our interview she discussed her psychopathic father and her siblings who used to burn down churches. Yet when I asked her, "What role did religion play in your early life?" she said, "I was deeply religious and I don't know whether you know it or not or whether I should even mention it [pause]. I think I better not because I begin to cry." This could have been an allusion to her father or siblings which she mentioned later in our interview. The pain in Paula's memory, coupled with the fact that she thought I was too young to understand, probably resulted in her not discussing some important formative events in her life.

Paula's reluctance was an exception. Answers to questions not directly related to my being a priest indicated that people were speaking honestly. For example, Helen was asked, "Is there anything that frightens you about the years ahead?" She replied, "I'm gonna tell you one dumb thing, really stupid, the most stupid thing I can think of, and I don't know how to overcome it—and that's I'm frightened of earthquakes. That's the only dumb thing." The fact that Helen would reveal "the most stupid thing" she could think of indicates a level of disclosure and trust in our interview.

One man seemed offended when I asked him, "I'm wondering if the fact that I'm a priest has...influenced our interview at all?" He replied quickly, "No, not one little bit. So, believe me, I set [sic] here and I opened my heart to you and I told you how I feel." In tone he seemed perturbed that I asked him the question. The impression I received was that the question was a betrayal of the honesty of his answers.

Despite these claims, the fact that I am a priest had influences on both the RCIA participants and the prayer group. At one RCIA meeting a young woman asked who I was and where I was from. I told her I was a priest from St. John's Seminary. Looking over my clothes, she said, "They let you out like that?" I replied, "Yeah, but the hard part is getting back in." In line during a refreshment break at the diocesan training session where I wore clerics, a woman in front of me stepped back to let me go ahead saying, "Collars first."

In arranging field visits to parish RCIA sessions, I coordinated visits with RCIA directors. One director asked me if I was going to wear clerics. When I told her no, she said the priests in her parish always do wear clerics and she would have to mention it to the pastor. She never mentioned the issue to me again.

At another parish I observed both the sponsor meeting and a meeting for new inquirers on the same evening. I told the director I wanted to remain anonymous. Yet at the sponsor meeting she introduced me as a priest and had me say a few words. I showed my surprise when she introduced me as "*Father* Rich Erikson." She said I did not have to be "incognito" with the sponsors. At the new inquirers meeting the fact that I was a priest was not mentioned.

In some field settings I remained completely anonymous. In others I was identified as a priest. At the diocesan RCIA training session I was introduced as a priest studying the RCIA. Thus the director told the gathering, "You may be in the study."

My interaction with the prayer group was more participatory than my interaction with RCIA members and meetings. The prayer group was meeting at a parish where I regularly said mass. Primarily because of my parish association, I did wear clerics when I observed the prayer group and when I interviewed the prayer group members. Before observing the group, I met with Sister Agnes and discussed with her my concern that there was a danger present that I may take on a "priestly role" in the group. To mitigate this possibility, I remained as passive and "in the background" as possible. Additionally, although I did wear clerics, I always wore bright or cardigan sweaters. In my field notes I came to refer to my prayer group outfits as my "Jimmy Carter Fireside Chat" outfits, recalling President Carter's effort to speak informally to the nation. Finally, I consistently deflected questions and concerns to Sister Agnes as the group leader. For example, when questions were asked in my direction, I would look directly at Sister Agnes for the answer.

When I interviewed Sister Agnes, I asked her about my presence in the group:

> *One thing we talked about before I sat in on the prayer group was my concern that my presence doesn't change the nature of the group or the interaction. Have you noticed any change?*
>
> No, I haven't.
>
> *The level of conversation hasn't changed or anything like that?*
>
> I haven't. Do you feel they are stiff or anything with you?
>
> *I don't think so.*
>
> They just think of you as part of the group. They don't think of you up here [drawing an imaginary pedestal in the air], Father, with all the answers. I think it's nice the way they sometimes refer

things to you, but it's like they would say it to whoever is in the line of vision. I think they feel very comfortable with you. I don't think it [your presence] has changed it [the group] at all.

The interactions detailed here, where the fact that I was a priest became evident, were probably indicative of other perceptions and attitudes that were not spoken. Yet, no matter if I were a baker or a Quaker, a woman or a foreman, I would have to deal with perceptions and attitudes. In weighing the pros and cons at the end of the project, I feel that being a priest had many benefits and costs. Yet, if I had presented myself as an anonymous researcher, there would have been as many, if not more, benefits and costs.

PERSONAL REFLECTIONS

Throughout the project there was a personal tension between being a priest and being a sociologist. My primary responsibility was to approach the study in a sociological and scientific manner. My observations and thoughts were primarily sociologically based. I thought and acted like the sociologist I am.

Yet, a few times I crossed the line which I had drawn between priest and sociologist. One difficult task was not to respond to statements made during the interview in a pastoral counseling mode and, at the same time, to use my pastoral counseling skills in a way which was conducive to the personal narratives being discussed.

Twice during interviews I abandoned the sociologist and became the priest when I was directly asked about a subject. Paula, the prayer group member, spoke of a dilemma she faced in that her closest friends were "anti-Catholic." She said: "But it bothers me that my closest friends are not religious. And I question sometimes, and talk to God about it: 'Should I do something about this?' My feeling is that I can't. I don't know whether that's right or wrong. Maybe you have some idea there?" I responded by suggesting that Paula trust in God and pray for her friends. This particular response, although a sociological mistake, is understandable given the nature of the prayer group. As mentioned, my participation in the prayer group was more closely linked to my being a priest. Additionally, not responding to her question may have contributed to her reluctance in the interview.

The second instance in which I "stepped over the sociological line" came in the interview with Joan. Once again I was directly asked to comment on a situation. Joan was discussing the fact that her daughter is a lesbian. She said, "It worries me to death." She added:

> But, y'know, I pray every night that she'll, y'know, get back in the church. And if I die, that's my biggest wish, for her to get back in the church, even though, now—If she should die, would she be saved or not, being a lesbian?

I responded that in my opinion a woman being a lesbian would not prevent her from being saved. I added that I thought salvation was open to anyone who chose to live with God for eternity. Finally I said we are beginning to learn that sexual orientation is not so much a conscious choice as it is a matter of biology.[2]

On three occasions I addressed some content of an interview after the interview was completed. During our interview one woman said she was confused about the church's teaching on the Trinity. I gave her my view on the Trinity on my way out. Another man also said he was confused about the Trinity and the use of incense. Again, as I moved to the door, I mentioned my views on each issue. Finally, I interviewed one woman on a day her infant granddaughter was in danger of dying. As I said goodbye, I said I would pray for her granddaughter. My sociological integrity remained intact since these three instances occurred after the interviews were completed. Other researchers may have responded in the same way.

On all other occasions during the interviews I did not address comments that may have been directed to me because I was a priest: comments such as, "I don't know how you feel about this," or, "I don't know what your theology is but...." Additionally, people felt comfortable enough with me to mention their disagreements with core Catholic teachings. The fact that I asked them if there were any Catholic teachings or beliefs that troubled them, or that they disagreed with, may have given them permission to discuss their disagreements. Through nodding my head, and not reacting negatively to what was being said, I allowed each person to speak of her/his convictions. Theologically some people said some things that I disagreed with, yet I never mentioned my disagreement. I feel I did not show any sign of my own disagreement.

Despite the already-mentioned research transgressions, I feel I played the researcher role well. I called on my research and interview skills, and called on my pastoral counseling skills only when they did not conflict with my research intent. Certainly, as a pastoral counselor, I have learned the vital necessity of letting people tell their stories. I have learned to listen and to engage in people's stories in such a way as to show my active interest and desire to hear more. My comfort in talking with people, my personal approach and style, and my pastoral counseling skills seemed to facilitate depth, trust, and honesty in our interviews. In the end, I feel the fact that I am a Catholic priest benefitted the study. By being a priest, I was able to communicate with and understand the people I interviewed in a unique and sociologically enhanced way.

Notes

1. I am grateful to D. Paul Johnson for his comments on a paper based on this appendix which was delivered at the annual meeting of the Association for the Sociology of Religion at Los Angeles, California, on August 5, 1994.

2. The entire interview with Joan was a near disaster. The temperature was over one hundred degrees outside and much warmer in Joan's house. Her house was in a rough neighborhood. As cars drove by during the interview, I wondered if one of them might be my car. The grass and shrubbery in her front yard was unkempt, as was Joan's appearance when she finally came to the door (after my ringing the doorbell and knocking at two different doors). I literally had to clear cobwebs to get through the door. The room we met in was decorated in dark brown. Joan kept the heavy brown curtains closed; I wondered if the curtains were originally white. Joan's speech was slurred. I speculated she was either heavily medicated or disoriented. She rarely directly addressed the questions I asked. I was with her for three hours, yet occasionally she would have moments of lucidity and insight.

Appendix B
The Sample, the Field Sites, and Roman Catholicism as a Context

Important characteristics of both the older new Catholics and the prayer group members were presented in the body of this book. Appendix B gives an in-depth presentation of the sample of older new Catholics, the RCIA field sites where observations were made, and addresses the question: "Why Roman Catholicism?"

OVERVIEW OF THE SAMPLE

The sample of twenty-eight individuals consisted of sixteen women and twelve men. They ranged in age, at the time of the interview, from fifty-eight years to eighty-one years.

TABLE 2: AGE OF RESPONDENTS IN YEARS AT TIME OF INTERVIEW

Age in Years	Number of Respondents
55–59	2
60–64	9
65–69	8
70–74	3
75–79	5
80–85	1

All but one respondent are American-born; the one exception is a Canadian-born man. All respondents are either currently married or have once been married. Of the 20 people who married once, 13 are still married and still living with their spouse, 3 are divorced, 2 are separated, and 2 are widowed. Of the 8 people who married twice, 6 are divorced and remarried, and 2 are widowed and remarried. There are two sets of individuals married to each other in the sample: one couple went through the RCIA together, and in the other, the wife completed the RCIA and the husband went through the process five years later.

TABLE 3: RESPONDENTS MARRIED ONCE

Marital Status	Number of Respondents
Still Married	13
Married but separated	2
Divorced	3
Widowed	2

TABLE 4: RESPONDENTS MARRIED TWICE

Marital Status	Number of Respondents
Divorced and remarried	6
Widowed and remarried	2

All but two of the respondents have children. Of the 13 still married people, 11 of the spouses are Catholic. Of the two married to non-Catholics, the woman married to a Lutheran became Catholic with her husband's support and encouragement. The woman who is married to a non-practicing Jew has a daughter who became Catholic and who significantly impacted her mother's decision to become Catholic. Recall that spousal and familial influences in the story of becoming Catholic are great.

Individuals were asked to categorize their "combined household income" as low, moderate, or high. The results of their self-reported income are as follows:

TABLE 5: SELF-REPORTED INCOME

Self-Reported Income	Number of Respondents
Low	4
Low-Moderate	3
Moderate	15
Moderate-High	1
High	5

All respondents live independently in their own, or in a rented, home, condominium, or apartment. One man is a Hollywood producer who lives in a lavish estate. One woman lives in a run-down neighborhood and has bars on the windows of her home. Another woman had to borrow money from the church in order to meet her rental payments.

Seventeen respondents spoke of their education in describing their personal histories.

TABLE 6: SELF-REPORTED LEVEL OF EDUCATIONAL ATTAINMENT

Self-Reported Level of Educational Attainment	Number of Respondents
Some high school	1
High school graduate	4
Some college	3
College graduate	7
Advanced degree	2
Unreported	11

Of the eleven people who did not discuss educational background, only one is in a profession that requires a college degree (teacher).

The respondents reported on their work status: 15 are retired, 2 are semi-retired, one had retired but has reentered the work force, one is on sick leave, 2 describe themselves as "housewife"; the remaining 7, who are not included in the categories above, are still working. The occupational backgrounds of the respondents are very diverse.

The religious backgrounds of the respondents' families at birth, or during their early childhood, were reported as follows:

TABLE 7: RELIGION OF EARLY CHILDHOOD HOUSEHOLD

Religion of Early Childhood Household	Number of Respondents
Mixed Protestant	5
None	4
Methodist	4
Mixed Catholic and Protestant	3
Baptist	3

Christian Science non-practicing	2
Presbyterian	2
Catholic	1
Broadly Protestant non-practicing	1
Lutheran	1
Pentecostal	1
Jewish	1

We can see, then, that the sample is relatively homogeneous. All had been, or are, married, all but one are American-born, all are Caucasian, all are living independently, all are over the age of fifty-eight, and all are living in Southern California. The homogeneity of the sample was only in part intended.

The intent of gathering a relatively homogeneous sample was to increase the generalizability of the findings to a relatively specialized population. Another criterion for selection that emerged as the study progressed was the desire to interview individuals at various stages in the RCIA process. Thus one RCIA director recommended two individuals who were not members of the Catholic Church but who were inquiring or seeking membership. One individual was interviewed three weeks after she approached the church about membership; the other individual was interviewed one year into the process. Additionally, a former Methodist minister seemed an attractive candidate to interview because of the uniqueness of the story and the recent date of his acceptance into the church.

The all-Caucasian, all-married nature of the sample was *not* by design. Although some respondents were interviewed because they were married, not all respondents were chosen to meet this criterion. The all-married nature of the sample can be accounted for, in part, by the importance of family as a motivator for joining the Catholic Church. Married individuals would have a greater likelihood of immediate family influence when compared to single individuals. An avenue for future research is to explore if people who join the Catholic Church in later life are overwhelmingly Caucasian, and, if so, to account for this phenomenon.

FIELD SITES

Field observations were made at the following sites:

(1) The first and second RCIA meetings of the new year in a parish. I observed both general presentations and small groups.

(2) A reunion of recently baptized Catholics. This meeting was a planning session for monthly educational meetings.

(3) RCIA Certification and Team Enrichment Session. This all-day training session was sponsored by a diocese for RCIA team leaders. The session was part of a series required by the diocese for one to become a certified catechist. The presentations were all related to the theme of adult faith development.

(4) RCIA Team Day. Again sponsored by a diocese, this all-day workshop included various presentations relating to practical issues of RCIA implementation and a worship service.

(5) A parish meeting of sponsors and catechumens. The particular focus of this weekly meeting was moral decision-making.

(6) A weekly parish meeting for new inquirers one month into the initiation process. The focus of this meeting was storytelling and the sharing of biographical transitions.

(7) A "debriefing" meeting of an RCIA team after a weekly meeting. The RCIA team spoke informally, evaluating attendance, participation, and the status of individual participants.

(8) A parish RCIA staff meeting. Particular issues relating to the development of the new class of participants and the sponsors were discussed.

(9) A liturgy conducted by a bishop to celebrate new Catholics (neophyte liturgy). Those who were baptized the previous year were recognized during the liturgy and honored at a reception following the mass.

(10) A retreat morning conducted by a parish RCIA director for those about to go through the Rite of Acceptance. The four-hour session focused on small-group activities and group prayer.

(11) A parish Rite of Acceptance. This ceremony marks the first step in the RCIA process. Both children and adults were formally accepted as catechumens by the parish.

(12) A seminary class for future priests. The course title was "Pastoral Catechetical Leadership." The two classes I observed focused on religious conversion and the RCIA.

(13) An Easter vigil liturgy at a parish. At this liturgy fifteen new Catholics were baptized, confirmed, and received their first communion; that is, they were fully initiated into the Catholic Church. An elderly new Catholic gave a witness talk after her baptism.

WHY ROMAN CATHOLICISM?

Lofland and Lofland advocate an approach to qualitative analysis whereby the researcher "starts where you are" (1984:7). Since I am a baptized Catholic and a priest, Roman Catholicism is certainly "where I am." My knowledge and experience as a Catholic, as a teacher for those seeking membership in the church, as a priest, and as the son of a convert provided depth to this project.

Roman Catholicism is an apt religion in which to study conversion and membership switching for a number of reasons. First, conversion literature focuses primarily on new religious movements and cults. A study of conversion to a "mainline" religion makes an important contribution to the sociology of religion.

Second, Roman Catholicism is not a religion that emphasizes a "born again" experience. Recruiting new members is not a prominent activity in the church. Infant baptisms are far more common than adult baptisms. Conversion literature has largely focused on adolescent and young adult conversion in "born again" religions. Given the emphasis in biographical reconstruction literature on the radical break with the past that religious conversion entails, the lack of emphasis on spontaneous and identifiable moments of religious conversion in Roman Catholicism seemed important to analyze.

Third, Roman Catholicism has been cited as a religion that attracts many new members for non-religious reasons. For example, many engaged couples are under the mistaken impression that the Catholic Church requires both individuals to be Catholic. Sometimes this mistaken impression is given by representatives of the church. Thus there is a non-religious incentive for interfaith marriage conversion. Additionally, the Catholic Church does instruct the Catholic partner of an interfaith marriage on the importance of teaching the Catholic faith to the children. Thus, many Catholics are encouraged to baptize their children Catholic. Again, a non-religious incentive for a non-Catholic to be baptized is present (that is, for the purpose of family harmony). Tamney summarizes: "Catholicism, in part because of its strong stand on children and its minimal standards for membership, attracts many converts little interested in the religious specifics of Catholicism" (1970:402).

An expectation of this research was that many of the "non-religious" reasons for joining the Catholic Church would not be present in the older new Catholics. Thus biographical reconstruction, which may or may not take a religious form, would be more frequent among older new Catholics. We found that this was not the case; however a focus on potential religious reasons for conversion to Roman Catholicism is another contribution to the field. Such a focus is in line with the perspective of William James (1961), who contends that in a religious conversion experience, religious ideas, which were previously peripheral in consciousness, now take a central place. Given the search for meaning in biographical reconstruction, I expected to discover religious ideas and meaning at the core of the efforts of older new Catholics to resolve life issues.

Fourth, Roman Catholicism is well-suited as a context for the social reconstruction of one's past. The tradition emphasized the importance of remembrance. The eucharist, the central focus of worship and belief for Catholics, entails the recalling of past events to find meaning for the present and hope for the future. These three elements—recalling, finding meaning and hope for the future—are also crucial elements in the life review process. Additionally, there is an autobiographical component built into the RCIA process.

Finally, this study provides a wider perspective for religious conversion theory (when compared to past studies that focused solely on young new religious movement converts) and a foundation for further study. Similar studies could be initiated with other religions or with Catholics in other parts of the world.

Bibliography

Adler, Herbert M. and Van Buren O. Hammett. 1973. "Crisis, Conversion, and Cult Formation: An Examination of A Common Psychosocial Sequence." *American Journal of Psychiatry* 130(8): 861–864.

Agostino, Joseph N. 1987. "Religiosity and Religious Participation in Later Years: A Reflection of the Spiritual Needs of the Elderly." *Journal of Religion and Aging* 4(2):75–82.

Albrecht, Stan L. and Marie Cornwall. 1989. "Life Events and Religious Change." *Review of Religious Research* 31(1):23–38.

Anderson, William A. 1986. *RCIA: A Total Parish Process: How to Implement the RCIA in Your Parish*. Dubuque, IA: William C. Brown.

Austin, Roy L. 1977. "Empirical Adequacy of Lofland's Conversion Model." *Review of Religious Research* 18(3)(Spring):282–287.

Babchuk, Nicholas et al. 1967. "Change in Religious Affiliation and Family Stability." *Social Forces* 45(4):551–555.

Back, Kurt W. (ed.). 1980. *Life Course: Integrative Theories and Exemplary Populations*. Boulder, CO: Westview Press.

Bainbridge, William Sims. 1992. "The Sociology of Conversion," pp. 178–191 in H. Newton Malony and Samuel Southard (eds.),

Handbook of Religious Conversion. Birmingham, AL: Religious Education Press.

Baltes, Paul and K. Warner Schaie (eds.). 1973. *Life-Span Development Psychology: Personality and Socialization.* New York: Academic Press.

Barker, Eileen. 1984. *The Making of a Moonie: Choice or Brainwashing?* New York: Basil Blackwell.

Barker, Irwin R. and Raymond F. Currie. 1985. "Do Converts Always Make the Most Committed Christians?" *Journal for the Scientific Study of Religion* 24(3):305–313.

Barros, Carmen. 1988. "Catholicism, Lifestyles, and the Wellbeing of the Elderly." *Journal of Religion and Aging* 4(3 and 4):109–118.

Beckford, James A. 1978. "Accounting for Conversion." *British Journal of Sociology* 29(2):249–262.

Bellah, Robert N. et al. 1985. *Habits of the Heart: Individualism and Commitment in American Life.* New York: Harper and Row.

Bengtson, Vern L. and James E. Birren (eds.). 1988. *Emergent Theories of Aging.* New York: Springer Publishing.

Berger, Peter. 1967. *The Sacred Canopy.* New York: Doubleday.

Berger, Peter and Brigitte Berger. 1972. *Sociology: A Biographical Approach.* New York: Basic Books.

Berger, Peter and Thomas Luckmann. 1967. *The Social Construction of Reality: A Treatise in the Sociology of Knowledge.* New York: Doubleday.

Berman, Harry J. 1991. "From the Pages of My Life." *Generations* 15(2):33–40.

Bertaux, Daniel (ed.). 1981. *Biography and Society: The Life History Approach in the Social Sciences.* Beverly Hills, CA: Sage Publications.

Bianchi, Eugene C. 1982. *Aging as a Spiritual Journey.* New York: Crossroad Publishing.

Birren, James E. 1964. *The Psychology of Aging.* Englewood Cliffs, NJ: Prentice-Hall.

Birren, James E. and Donna E. Deutchman. 1991. *Guiding Autobiography Groups for Older Adults.* Baltimore: Johns Hopkins University Press.

Blazer, Dan. 1992. "When Meaning Crumbles: Spiritual Integration and Emotional Concerns." Keynote Address, Aging and the Emerging Spirit Conference Sponsored by the American Society on Aging Forum on Religion and Aging. San Diego, CA. March 13, 1992.

Blazer, Dan and Erdman Palmore. 1976. "Religion and Aging in a Longitudinal Panel." *Gerontologist* 16 (1): 82–85.

Botella, Luis and Feixas Guillem. 1993. "The Autobiographical Group: A Tool for the Reconstruction of Past Life Experience with the Aged." *International Journal of Aging and Human Development* 36(4):303–319.

Briggs, Charles L. 1989. *Learning How to Ask: A Socio-linguistic Appraisal of the Role of the Interview in Social Science Research.* Cambridge, England: Cambridge University Press.

Buhler, Charlotte. 1935. "The Curve of Life as Studied in Biographies." *The Journal of Applied Psychology* 19:405–409.

Butler, Robert N. 1963. "The Life Review: An Interpretation of Reminiscence in the Aged."*Psychiatry* 26:65–76.

———. 1971. "Age: The Life Review." *Psychology Today* 5(7):49–51, 89.

———. 1974. "Successful Aging and the Life Review." *Journal of the American Geriatric Society* 22 (12):529–535.

———. 1975. *Why Survive? Being Old in America.* New York: Harper and Row.

———. 1980–1981. "The Life Review: An Unrecognized Bonanza." *International Journal of Aging and Human Development* 12(1): 35–38.

Butler, Robert N. and Myrna I. Lewis. 1974. "Life Review Therapy: Putting Memories to Work in Individual and Group Psychotherapy." *Geriatrics* 29(11):165–173.

Chubon, Sandra. 1980. "A Novel Approach to the Process of Life Review." *Journal of Gerontological Nursing* 6(9):543–546.

Clausen, John A. 1972. "The Life Course of Individuals," pp. 457–514 in Matilda Riley White et al. (eds.), *Aging and Society Volume Three: A Sociology of Age Stratification.* New York: Russell Sage Foundation.

Cohler, Bertram J. 1982. "Personal Narrative and Life Course," pp. 205–241 in Paul B. Baltes and Orvile G. Brim, Jr. (eds.), *Life-Span Development and Behavior: Volume Four.* New York: Academic Press.

Conn, Walter E. 1986. "Adult Conversions." *Pastoral Psychology* 34(4)(Summer):225–236.

Corbin, Juliet and Anselm Strauss. 1990. "Grounded Theory Research: Procedures, Canons, and Evaluative Criteria." *Qualitative Sociology* 13(1):3–21.

Cox, Harold and Andre Hammonds. 1988. "Religiosity, Aging, and Life Satisfaction." *Journal of Religion and Aging* 5(1 and 2):1–21.

Creen, Edward and Henry Simmons. 1977. "Toward an Understanding of Religious Needs in Aging Persons." *The Journal of Pastoral Care* 31(4):273–278.

DeMaria, Richard. 1978. "A Psycho-Social Analysis of Religious Conversion," pp. 82–130 in M. Darrol Bryant and Herbert W. Richardson (eds.), *A Time for Consideration: A Scholarly*

Appraisal of the Unification Church. New York: Edwin Mellen Press.

Denzin, Norman K. 1989. *Interpretive Biography.* Newbury Park, CA: Sage Publications.

Disch, Robert (ed.). 1988. *Twenty-Five Years of the Life Review: Theoretical and Practical Considerations.* New York: Haworth Press.

Duggan, Robert D. (ed). 1984a. *Conversion and the Catechumenate.* New York: Paulist Press.

———. 1984b "Sociological Perspectives on Conversion," pp. 120–144 in Robert D. Duggan (ed.), *Conversion and the Catechumenate.* New York: Paulist Press.

———. 1989. "A Response to Andrew M. Greeley." *America* 161(10): 235–237.

Dunning, James B. 1979. "The Rite of Christian Initiation of Adults: Model of Adult Growth." *Worship* 53(2):142–156.

———. 1981a. *New Wine, New Wineskins: Exploring the RCIA.* New York: William H. Sadlier.

———. 1981b. "The Stages of Initiation: I. Inquiry," pp. 177–197 in William J. Reedy (ed.), *Becoming a Catholic Christian: A Symposium on Christian Initiation.* New York: William H. Sadlier.

Durkheim, Emile. 1976. *The Elementary Forms of the Religious Life.* 2nd ed. London: George Allen and Unwin.

Elder, Glen. 1981. "History and the Life Course," pp. 77–115 in Daniel Bertaux (ed.), *Biography and Society: The Life History Approach in the Social Sciences.* Beverly Hills, CA: Sage Publications.

Ellis, John Tracy. 1976. "Conversions in American Catholic History," pp. 159–163 in Robert Trisco (ed.), *Catholics in America: 1776–1976.* Washington, D.C.: National Conference of Catholic Bishops.

Emerson, Robert M. (ed.). 1983. *Contemporary Field Research: A Collection of Readings.* Prospect Heights, IL: Waveland Press.

Erikson, Erik H. 1968. *Identity and the Life Cycle.* New York: W. W. Norton.

———. 1975. *Life History and the Historical Moment.* New York: W. W. Norton.

———. 1982. *The Life Cycle Completed: A Review.* New York: W. W. Norton.

Ferrel, Carolyn et al. 1988. "Religion and Well-Being in Later Life." *The Gerontologist* 28(1):18–28.

Fichter, Joseph H. 1987. *Autobiographies of Conversion.* Lewiston, New York/Queenston, Ontario: Edwin Mellen.

Friedan, Betty. 1993. *The Fountain of Age.* New York: Simon and Schuster.

Gartrell, C. David and Zane K. Shannon. 1985. "Contacts, Cognitions, and Conversion: A Rational Choice Approach." *Review of Religious Research* 27(1):32–48.

Georgemiller, Randy J. and Stephen H. Getsinger. 1987. "Reminiscence Therapy: Effects on More and Less Religious Elderly." *Journal of Religion and Aging* 4(2):47–58.

Gillespie, V. Bailey. 1979. *Religious Conversion and Personal Identity: How and Why People Change.* Birmingham, AL: Religious Education Press.

———. 1991. *The Dynamics of Religious Conversion: Identity and Transformation.* Birmingham, AL: Religious Education Press.

Greeley, Andrew M. 1989. "Against R.C.I.A." *America* 161(10):231–234.

Hadaway, Christopher Kirk. 1978. "Denominational Switching and

Membership Growth: In Search of A Relationship." *Sociological Analysis* 39(4):321–337.

———. 1980. "Denominational Switching and Religiosity." *Review of Religious Research* 21 Supp. (4):451–461.

Haight, Barbara K. 1989a. "Life Review: A Method of Pastoral Counseling: Part I." *Journal of Religion and Aging* 5(3):17–29.

———. 1989b. "Life Review: A Report of the Effectiveness of a Structured Life Review Process: Part II." *Journal of Religion and Aging* 5(3):31–41.

———. 1992. "Long-Term Effects of a Structured Life Review Process." *The Journals of Gerontology* 47(5): P312–P315.

Hamberg, Eva M. 1991. "Stability and Change in Religious Beliefs, Practice, and Attitudes: A Swedish Panel Study." *Journal for the Scientific Study of Religion* 30(1):63–80.

Hareven, Tamara K. 1980. "The Life Course and Aging in Historical Perspective," pp. 9–25 in Kurt W. Back (ed.), *Life Course: Integrative Theories and Exemplary Populations.* Boulder, CO: Westview Press.

Harms, Ernest. 1962. "Ethical and Psychological Implications of Religious Conversion." *Review of Religious Research* 3(3): 122–131.

Hateley, B. J. 1984. "Spiritual Well-Being Through Life Histories." *Journal of Religion and Aging* 1(2):63–71.

Heirich, Max. 1977. "Change of Heart: A Test of Some Widely Held Theories about Religious Conversion." *American Journal of Sociology* 83(3):653–680.

Hiltner, Seward. 1966. "Toward a Theology of Conversion in Light of Psychology." *Pastoral Psychology* 17:35–42.

Hoge, Dean R. et al. 1981. *Converts, Dropouts, Returnees: A Study of Religious Change Among Catholics.* New York: Pilgrim Press.

Howe, Leroy T. 1979. "A Developmental Perspective on Conversion." *Perkins Journal* 33(Fall):20–35.

James, William. 1961. *The Varieties of Religious Experience: A Study in Human Nature.* New York: Macmillan.

Johnson, Malcolm. 1978. "That Was Your Life: A Biographical Approach to Later Life," pp. 99–116 in Vida Carver and Penny Liddiard (eds.), *An Ageing Population.* Kent, Great Britain: Hodder and Stoughton in association with The University Press.

Johnson, Paul E. 1959. "Conversion." *Pastoral Psychology* 10(95): 51–56.

Johnson, Paul R. 1976. "Society, Knowledge and Religion: The Perspective of Peter Berger." *Perspectives in Religious Studies* 3:291–304.

Kaminsky, Marc. 1984. "The Uses of Reminiscence: A Discussion of the Formative Literature." *Journal of Gerontological Social Work* 7(1 and 2):137–156.

Kemp, Raymond B. 1979. *A Journey in Faith: An Experience of the Catechumenate.* New York: William H. Sadlier.

Kilbourne, Brock and James T. Richardson. 1989. "Paradigm Conflict, Types of Conversion, and Conversion Theories." *Sociological Analysis* 50(1):1–21.

Kimble, Melvin A. 1990. "Aging and the Search for Meaning." *Journal of Religious Gerontology* 7(1 and 2):111–129.

Koenig, Harold G. et al. 1989. "Religious and Non-Religious Coping: Impact on Adaption in Later Life." *Journal of Religion and Aging* 5(4):73–94.

———. 1988. "Religion and Well-Being in Later Life." *The Gerontologist* 28(1):18–28.

Kohli, Martin. 1981. "History and the Life Course," pp. 61–75 in Daniel

Bertaux (ed.), *Biography and Society: The Life History Approach in the Social Sciences.* Beverly Hills, CA: Sage Publications.

Krefting, Laura. 1991. "Rigor in Qualitative Research: The Assessment of Trustworthiness." *The American Journal of Occupational Therapy* 45(3):214–222.

Lamme, Simone and Jan Baars. 1993. "Including Social Factors in the Analysis of Reminiscence in Elderly Individuals." *International Journal of Aging and Human Development* 37(4):297–311.

Leininger, C. Earl. 1975. "The Dynamics of Conversion: Toward a Working Model." *Perspectives in Religious Studies* 2(2):190–201.

Levin, Jeffrey S. 1988. "Religious Factors in Aging, Adjustment, and Health: A Theoretical Overview," pp. 133–146 in William Clements (ed.), *Religions, Aging and Health: A Global Perspective.* New York: Hawthorne Press.

Lewis, Charles N. 1971. "Reminiscing and Self–Concept in Old Age." *Journal of Gerontology* 26(2):240–243.

Lieberman, M. A. and Jacqueline M. Falk. 1971. "The Remembered Past as a Source of Data for Research on the Life Cycle." *Human Development* 14(2):132–141.

Linn, Margaret W. 1973. "Perceptions of Childhood: Present Functioning and Past Events." *Journal of Gerontology* 28(2): 202–206.

Liu, William T. and Nathaniel J. Pallone. 1970. *Catholics/U.S.A.: Perspectives on Social Change.* New York: John Wiley and Sons.

Lofland, John. 1966. *Doomsday Cult: A Study of Conversion, Proselytization and Maintenance of Faith.* Englewood Cliffs, NJ: Prentice-Hall.

Lofland, John and Lyn H. Lofland. 1984. *Analyzing Social Settings: A Guide to Qualitative Observation.* 2nd ed. Belmont, CA: Wadsworth Publishing.

Lofland, John and Norman Skonovd. 1981. "Conversion Motifs." *Journal for the Scientific Study of Religion* 20(4):373–385.

Lofland, John and Rodney Stark. 1965. "Becoming a World-saver: A Theory of Conversion to a Deviant Perspective." *American Sociological Review* 30(6):862–875.

Long, Theodore and Jeffrey Hadden. 1983. "Religious Conversion and the Concept of Socialization: Integrating the Brainwashing and Drift Models." *Journal for the Scientific Study of Religion* 22(1):1–14.

Luckmann, Thomas. 1967. *The Invisible Religion.* New York: Macmillan.

Malony, H. Newton and Samuel Southard (eds.). 1992. *Handbook of Religious Conversion.* Birmingham, AL: Religious Education Press.

McAllister, Ian. 1988. "Religious Change and Secularization: The Transmission of Religious Values in Australia." *Sociological Analysis* 49(3):249–262.

Mead, George H. 1963. *The Philosophy of the Present.* A. Murphy (ed.), Lasalle, IL: Open Court.

Merriam, Sharan B. 1993. "Butler's Life Review: How Universal Is It?" *International Journal of Aging and Human Development* 37(3):163–175.

Mick, Lawrence E. 1989. *RCIA: Renewing the Church as an Initiating Assembly.* Collegeville, MN: Liturgical Press.

Mishler, Elliot G. 1986. *Research Interviewing: Context and Narrative.*Cambridge, MA: Harvard University Press.

Molinari, Victor and Robert E. Reichlin. 1984–1985. "Life Review Reminiscence in the Elderly: A Review of the Literature."

International Journal of Aging and Human Development 20(2): 81–92.

Moody, Harry R. 1988. "Twenty-Five Years of the Life Review: Where Did We Come From? Where Are We Going?" pp. 7–21 in Robert Disch (ed.), *Twenty-Five Years of the Life Review: Theoretical and Practical Considerations.* New York: Haworth Press.

Morse, Claire K. and Patricia A. Wisocki. 1987. "Importance of Religiosity to Elderly Adjustment." *Journal of Religion and Aging* 4(1):15–26.

Morycz, Richard K. 1980. "Formative Perspectives on Life Review and Pastoral Counseling for the Elderly." *Studies in Formative Spirituality* 1(3):379–392.

Moseley, Romney M. 1984. "Faith Development and Conversion in the Catechumenate," pp. 145–163 in Robert D. Duggan (ed.), *Conversion and the Catechumenate.* New York: Paulist Press.

Myerhoff, Barbara. 1978. *Number Our Days.* New York: Simon and Schuster.

———. 1980. "Life History Among the Elderly: Performance, Visibility and Re-Membering," pp. 135–155 in Kurt W. Back (ed.), *Life Course: Integrative Theories and Exemplary Populations.* Boulder, CO: Westview Press.

Nelson, E. Anne and Dale Dannefer. 1992. "Aged Heterogeneity: Fact or Fiction? The Fate of Diversity in Gerontological Research." *The Gerontologist* 32(1):17–23.

Neugarten, Bernice L. and Nancy Datan. 1973. "Sociological Perspectives on the Life Cycle," pp. 53–69 in Paul B. Baltes and K. Warner Schaie (eds.), *Life-Span Developmental Psychology: Personality and Socialization.* New York: Academic Press.

Newport, Frank. 1979. "The Religious Switcher in the United States." *American Sociological Review* 44(4):528–552.

Oakham, Ron. 1993. "Q and A." *Christian Initiation* August/ September, 1993.

Olszewski, Daryl. 1991. *Memories of the Journey: An RCIA Remembrance Book*. Milwaukee: Hi-Time Publishing.

O'Rourke, David K. 1987. "The Experience of Conversion," pp. 1–30 in Francis A. Eigo (ed.), in *The Human Experience of Conversion: Persons and Structures in Transformation*. Villanova, PA: Villanova University Press.

Parker, James V. 1981. "The Stages of Initiation: Part III. Purification and Enlightenment," pp. 219–229 in William J. Reedy (ed.), *Becoming a Christian: A Symposium on Christian Initiation*. New York: William H. Sadlier.

Parrucci, Dennis J. 1968. "Religious Conversion: A Theory of Deviant Behavior." *Sociological Analysis* 29(3):144–154.

Payne, Barbara. 1990a. "Spiritual Maturity and Meaning-Filled Relationships: A Sociological Perspective." *Journal of Religious Gerontology* 7(1 and 2):25–39.

Payne, Barbara Pittard. 1990b. "Research and Theoretical Approaches to Spirituality and Aging." *Generations: Quarterly Journal of the American Society on Aging*. 14(4):11–14.

Proudfoot, Wayne. 1985. *Religious Experience*. Berkeley: University of California Press.

Proudfoot, Wayne and Phillip Shaver. 1975. "Attribution Theory and the Psychology of Religion." *Journal for the Scientific Study of Religion* 14(4):317–330.

Rambo, Lewis R. 1993. *Understanding Religious Conversion*. New Haven, CT: Yale University Press.

RCIA Starter Stories: Volume One and Two. 1991. (Video Tapes) Liguori, MO: Liguori Publications.

Reedy, William J. (ed.). 1981. *Becoming a Catholic Christian: A Symposium on Christian Initiation.* New York: William H. Sadlier.

Reminiscence: Finding Meaning in Memories, Resource Materials. 1989. Washington, D.C.: American Association of Retired Persons.

Revere, Virginia and Sheldon S. Tobin. 1980–81. "Myth and Reality: the Older Person's Relationship to His Past." *International Journal of Aging and Human Development* 12(1):15–26.

Richardson, James T. 1985. "The Active vs. Passive Convert: Paradigm Conflict in Conversion/Recruitment Research." *Journal for the Scientific Study of Religion* 24(2):163–179.

Richardson, James T. et al. 1979. *Organized Miracles.* New Brunswick, NJ: Transaction.

Rite of Christian Initiation of Adults: Study Edition. 1988. New York: Catholic Book Publishing.

Ritzer, George. 1981. *Toward an Integrated Sociological Paradigm.* Boston: Allyn and Bacon.

Roof, Wade Clark and Dean Hoge. 1980. "Church Involvement in America: Social Factors Affecting Membership and Participation." *Review of Religious Research* 21(4):405–426.

Roof, Wade Clark and William McKinney. 1987. *American Mainline Religion: Its Changing Shape and Future.* New Brunswick, NJ: Rutgers University Press.

Roozen, David A. 1980. "Church Dropouts: Changing Patterns of Disengagement and Re-entry." *Review of Religious Research* 21(4):427–450.

Rosten, Leo. 1975. "Intermarriage—Statistics, Opinions, and Conversion Data: Catholics, Protestants and Jews," pp. 549–562 in Leo Rosten (ed.), *Religions of America: Ferment and Faith in an Age of Crisis.* New York: Simon and Schuster.

Ryan, John K., translator. 1960. *The Confessions of St. Augustine.* Garden City, New York: Image Books.

Salisbury, W. Seward. 1969. "Religious Identification, Mixed Marriage and Conversion." *Journal for the Scientific Study of Religion* 8(1):125–129.

Schutz, Alfred. 1962. *Collected Papers: Volume One.* The Hague: Nijhoff.

Seggar, John and Phillip Kunz. 1972. "Conversion: Evaluation of a Step-like Process for Problem Solving." *Review of Religious Research* 13(3):178–184.

Shannon, Zane K. 1985. "Contracts, Cognitions, Conversion: A Rational Choice Approach." *Review of Religious Research* 27(1):32–48.

Sherman, Edmund. 1991. *Reminiscence and the Self in Old Age.* New York: Springer Publishing Company.

Snizek, William E. et al. (eds.). 1979. *Contemporary Issues in Theory and Research: A Metasociological Perspective.* Westport, CT: Greenwood Press.

Snow, David A. and Cynthia Phillips. 1980. "The Lofland–Stark Conversion Model: A Critical Reassessment." *Social Problems* 27(4):430–447.

Snow, David A. and Richard Machalek. 1983. "The Convert as a Social Type," pp. 259–282 in Randall Collins (ed.), *Sociological Theory 1983.* San Francisco: Jossey-Bass Publishers.

———. 1984. "The Sociology of Conversion." *Annual Reviews in Sociology* 10:167–190.

Staples, Clifford L. and Armand L. Mauss. 1987. "Conversion or Commitment? A Reassessment of the Snow and Machalek Approach to the Study of Conversion." *Journal for the Scientific Study of Religion* 26(2):133–147.

Straus, Roger. 1976. "Changing Oneself: Seekers and the Creative

Transformation of Life Experience," pp. 252–272 in John Lofland (ed.), *Doing Social Life: The Qualitative Study of Human Interaction in Natural Settings.* New York: John Wiley and Sons.

Straus, Roger A. 1979. "Religious Conversion as a Personal and Collective Accomplishment." *Sociological Analysis* 40(2):158–165.

Strauss, Anselm L. 1989. *Qualitative Analysis for Social Scientists.* Cambridge, England: Cambridge University Press.

Strauss, Anselm and Juliet Corbin. 1990. *Basics of Qualitative Research: Grounded Theory, Procedures and Techniques.* New York: Sage Publications.

Suchman, Mark C. 1992. "Analyzing the Determinants of Everyday Conversion." *Sociological Analysis.* 53(S): S15–S33.

Tamney, Joseph B. 1970. "The Social Psychology of Conversion," pp. 399–418 in William T. Liu and Nathaniel J. Pallone (eds.), *Catholics U.S.A.: Perspectives on Social Change.* New York: John Wiley and Sons.

Taylor, Brian. 1978. "Recollection and Membership: Converts' Talk and the Ratiocination of Commonality." *Sociology: The Journal of the British Sociological Association* 12(2):316–324.

Taylor, Bryan. 1976. "Conversion and Cognition: An Area for Empirical Study in the Microsociology of Religious Knowledge." *Social Compass* 23(1):5–22.

Taylor, Robert Joseph and Linda M. Chatters. 1991. "Nonorganizational Religious Participation Among Elderly Black Adults." *The Journals of Gerontology* 46(2):S103–S111.

The Official Catholic Directory: Anno Domini 1994. 1994. Wilmette, IL: P. J. Kennedy and Sons.

Thomas, W. I. and Florian Znaniecki. 1927. *The Polish Peasant in Europe and America: Monograph of an Immigrant Group.* 2nd ed. New York: Alfred Knopf.

Thomason, Burke C. 1982. *Making Sense of Reification: Alfred Schutz and Constructionist Theory.* Atlantic Highlands, NJ: Humanities Press.

Throop, John R. 1986. "America's Catholics: Why Some Stay, Why Others Leave." *Christianity Today.* 30(16):31–33.

Trisco, Robert (ed.). 1976. *Catholics in America: 1776–1976.* Washington, D.C.: National Conference of Catholic Bishops.

Tucker, Robert C. (ed.). 1978. *The Marx-Engels Reader.* 2nd ed. New York: W. W. Norton.

Ullman, Chana. 1989. *The Transformed Self: The Psychology of Religious Conversion.* New York: Plenum Press.

Wallace, J. Brandon. 1992. "Reconsidering the Life Review: The Social Construction of Talk About the Past." *The Gerontologist* 32(1):120–125.

Wallace, Ruth A. 1975. "A Model of Change of Religious Affiliation." *Journal for the Scientific Study of Religion* 14(4):345–355.

Walrath, Douglas Alan. 1980. "Why Some People May Go Back to Church." *Review of Religious Research* 21(4):468–475.

Weber, Max. 1946. *From Max Weber: Essays in Sociology.* Eds. H. H. Gerth and C. Wright Mills. New York: Oxford University Press.

———. 1949. *The Methodology of the Social Sciences.* Trans. and eds. Edward A. Shils and Henry A. Finch. New York: Free Press of Glencoe.

Welsh, John F. 1983. "Beyond Berger and Luckmann: Toward a Praxis-Oriented Sociology of Knowledge." *Quarterly Journal of Ideology* 7(1):66–69.

White, Matilda Riley et al. (eds.). 1972. *Aging and Society Volume Three: A Sociology of Age Stratification.* New York: Russell Sage Foundation.

Willits, Fern K. and Donald Crider. 1989. "Church Attendance and Traditional Religious Beliefs in Adolescence and Young Adulthood: A Panel Study." *Review of Religious Research* 31(1):68–81.

Wuthnow, Robert J. 1988. "Sociology of Religion." pp. 473–509 in Neil J. Smelser (ed.), *Handbook of Sociology*. Newbury Park, CA: Sage Publications.

Yinger, J. Milton. 1967. "Pluralism, Religion, and Secularism." *Journal for the Scientific Study of Religion* 6:17–28.

———. 1969. "A Structural Examination of Religion." *Journal for the Scientific Study of Religion* 8:88–99.

Zetterberg, Hans. 1952. "The Religious Conversion as a Change of Social Roles." *Sociology and Social Research* 36:159–166.

Index

Anderson, William, 35, 113, 116, 138
Arn, Charles, 88
Augustine, Saint, 7

Babchuk, Nicholas, 136
Bainbridge, William Sims, 154, 156
Ballweg, John, 136
Barker, Eileen, 135
Baras, Jan, 15
Beckford, James, 27, 153, 155
Bellah, Robert, 10, 131
Berger, Brigitte, 11, 80
Berger, Peter, 1, 11-12, 16-20, 36, 38-40, 54, 63, 65-66, 68, 75-76, 80, 85-86, 88-89, 94, 102, 104-105, 108-110, 115, 119-122, 128, 135-139, 151-152
Berman, Harry, 5
Bertaux, Daniel, 9
Birren, James, 88-89
Blazer, Dan, 141
Butler, Robert, 1, 11, 13-17, 19, 28, 41, 156

Carter, James Earl, 164

Clausen, John, 80
Cohler, Bertram, 96, 105
Creen, Edward, 15
Crockett, Harry, 136

Datan, Nancy, 122, 148
de Beauvoir, Simone, 15
Denzin, Norman, 10
Deutchman, Donna, 88-89
Draper, Elaine, 2
Duggan, Robert, 19, 148
Dunning, James, 21-22, 34-36, 74, 82, 102-103, 125, 143
Durkheim, Emile, 16

Elder, Glen, 10
Erikson, Erik, 59, 81, 99, 105

Freud, Sigmund, 105
Friedan, Betty, 3

Gartrell, C. David, 152
Gillespie, V. Bailey, 28
Greeley, Andrew, 29, 132

Hadaway, Christopher Kirk, 26
Hadden, Jeffrey, 94
Haight, Barbara, 15

Index

Heirich, Max, 23, 105, 151
Hoge, Dean, 20, 81, 88, 99, 105, 119, 132
Homans, George, 10

James, William, 11-12, 149, 174
Johnson, D. Paul, 167

Kelly, Dean, 154
Kemp, Raymond, 65, 125
Kilbourne, Brock, 81, 116, 143
Kohli, Martin, 10
Kunz, Phillip, 132

Lamme, Simone, 15
Levin, Jeffrey, 149
Lofland, John, 94, 173
Lofland, Lyn, 173
Long, Theodore, 94
Luckmann, Thomas, 1, 11-12, 16-20, 36, 38-40, 54, 63, 65-66, 68, 75-76, 85-86, 88-89, 94, 102, 104-105, 108-110, 115, 119-122, 128, 135-139, 151-152

Machalek, Richard, 11-13, 18, 24, 28, 38, 40, 54, 148, 150
Mahony, Roger Cardinal, 30
Mannheim, Karl, 29
Mauss, Armand, 13, 28, 29
McAllister, Ian, 99
McKinney, William, 26
Mead, George Herbert, 16, 18
Merriam, Sharan, 15
Mick, Lawrence, 21, 27
Miller, Don, 2
Miller, Jon, 2
Moody, Harry, 10, 15

Morycz, Richard, 15
Murphy, Sister Ann Veronica, 2
Myerhoff, Barbara, 29

Neugarten, Bernice, 122, 148

Oakham, Ron, 8
O'Rourke, David, 34-35, 87-88, 113, 136-137, 147

Parker, James, 34
Parrucci, Dennis, 104-105
Paul VI, Pope, 30
Phillips, Cynthia, 12, 38, 52
Proudfoot, Wayne, 29

Rambo, Lewis, 155
Richardson, James, 81, 116, 143, 145, 147
Ritzer, George, 18
Roof, Wade Clark, 26, 99, 105, 119
Ryan, John, 7

Schutz, Alfred, 16, 121
Seegar, John, 132
Shannon, Zane, 152
Simmons, Andre, 15
Snizek, William, 18
Snow, David, 11-13, 18, 24, 28, 38, 40, 52, 148, 150
Staples, Clifford, 13, 28, 29
Stark, Rodney, 94, 111
Straus, Roger, 18-19, 28
Suchman, Mark, 28, 146

Tamney, Joseph, 173-174
Taylor, Brian, 12
Taylor, Bryan, 148

Thomas, W. I., 9-10
Throop, John, 132

Ullman, Chana, 105

Wallace, J. Brandon, 15, 156
Weber, Max, 16, 119, 155, 156

Znaniecki, Florian, 9